# OLD CROW

By Arthur Garrett

Copyright © 2021 Garrett A. Steiner
**All Rights Reserved**

No part of this book may be reproduced or transmitted in any form or by any means, electronic or mechanical. This includes photocopying or recording by any information storage or retrieval system, without written permission from the author.

Garrett A Steiner
steinerga@aol.com

Garrett A Steiner, 2021
1. Alcoholism—PTSD. 2. Abuse—Self-sacrifice. 3. Family relationships. 4. Childhood antics--humorous situations. 5. Memoir--United States.

p. 114
ISBN 978-0-578-95417-2 (print)
ISBN 978-0-578-95418-9 (e-book)

SUMMARY: post-WWII story about two boys growing up with a war-hero father ravished by PTSD, which he liberally self-medicated with alcohol precipitating flaming, uncontrollable alcoholism, and prodigious violence. The heartbreak of their day-to-day existence is moderated by their antics as they are joined by their aunt of the same age at their safe place: Grandma's house.

Cover Design: by Jen Aiken (jen@jvodesign.com)
Cover Photo: Google stock, non-proprietary

The paper used in this publication meets the requirements of the American National Standard for Permanence of Paper for Printed Library Materials Z39.48-1984.First edition.
Printed in the United States of America.

*All events described in this true story are life experiences of the author. Some characters in his story are not identified by their actual names.*

# ABOUT OLD CROW

*Old Crow* is a post-WWII story about two boys growing up with a war-hero father ravished by PTSD, which he liberally self-medicated with alcohol precipitating flaming, uncontrollable alcoholism and prodigious violence. The heartbreak of their day-to-day existence is moderated by their antics as they're joined by their aunt of the same age at their safe place: Grandma's house. Finally, the bravery and love of their mother, who mitigated the daily violence with self-sacrifice, is nothing short of inspirational. The ongoing tragedy of WWII was the men who spent a lifetime trying turn off the war still raging in their minds. In fact, alcoholism was all too common as these war heroes used the only drug, readily available, to numb their emotional pain.

# CONTENTS

# - 1 -
## THE DUFFY PLACE

The Duffy Place, the safe place, was a run-down two-story clapboard farmhouse north of Perry, Oklahoma. The Duffy Place is where my brother Red and I stayed, along with my baby sister Carlene, when things got so bad at home we needed a safe place. I was five, Red was seven, and my baby sister was still in diapers. At the Duffy place we connected with my mother's family: our Granddad (Coyote), Grandma (Mom), Aunt Yvonne, who is our age, and our Uncles Billy and Teddy, who are 10 and 12 years our senior, respectively. We were always happy to be there and relieved to leave our nomadic life as we moved from town to town as our father pursued the 'perfect job.'

The Duffy Place was in a total state of disrepair. In fact, there were boards missing on both porches. The screen door on the back porch had holes big enough to throw a cat through. A giant wood stove graced the center of the house, strategically placed just beyond the archway into the living room.

Billy and Teddy had a huge pin out back where they kept raccoons, coyotes, opossums, owls, or whatever critter they could catch. Yvonne had a pet opossum she called Baby-O. Teddy had two raccoons that were meaner than snakes and would attack without provocation. We knew to stay away from them, but they would not leave us alone. In fact, they would crawl around on us, reaching into our pockets for treats. The yard was scraped down to bare ground by a duke's mixture of chickens and hound dogs. During the hot, dry summer, the chickens would carve out dust wallows in the dry powdery soil as a means of controlling lice and cooling themselves. Also, there were several hens with chicks, and getting too close to them would get you a nasty flogging. One morning, Red and I were startled awake by the crack of a rifle. We were told the standoffish black and tan farm dog with bushy hair, pointed ears, and one blue and one yellow eye, went crazy from a snake bite and had to be shot. More than likely, the dog had rabies and we were lucky we weren't bitten.

There was a big hay barn full of small square bales of prairie hay. It had a loft and a rope swing lashed to the rafters by my Uncle Teddy. There was no question, Teddy was King of the Barn. He made tunnels through the hay and built secret rooms throughout. Yvonne and Red considered me the third wheel and frequently hid from me in a one-sided game of hide and seek. When they came out of hiding, we took turns on the rope swing. When Teddy came to the barn with us, which rarely happened, we were mesmerized by his prowess on the rope swing and how quickly he could disappear into one of his secret tunnels in the hay. He would rescue me from Red and Yvonne, when they began teasing me, carrying me blissfully on his shoulders. I know now that he is all of 5' 7" but as a child, to me, he was a brawny giant. He called me Frog Eyes, which he frequently shortened to froggy. He would say, "Come on, Froggy, you can go with me," as he swung me onto his shoulders.

For three mischievous kids on their own, the Duffy Place provided freedom for us to steep ourselves in one adventure after another, some of which became misadventures. Sometimes we would go to the big pond with Mom where she would fish with a 12-foot cane pole. We were always on an adventure and barely had time to stop for meals. Mom never worried about us. She would say, "They'll show up when they get hungry." She would cover leftovers with dish towels and leave them on the table, not especially sanitary by today's standards. However, we were always happy to find food waiting for us when we breezed in from our latest adventure.

Mom was very superstitious, and on rare occasions when we went to town, if a black cat crossed her path she would turn around and go home. We could not urge her, harass her, or shame her into doing otherwise. She would say, "You kids shut up now. It isn't worth the risk. I will kill one of the old hens and make some egg noodles." With a jersey cow grazing in the small pasture by the hay barn and a yard full of chickens. Mom could always pull together a meal for the six of us. Despite, her persistent limp, and frequent urinary needs, precipitated by her miniscule bladder, she busied herself about making butter, cottage cheese and buttermilk, coyotes favorite. Also, her chickens made great table fair, and our mother would show up frequently with sacks of groceries to contribute to the larder.

When Billy or Teddy drove us to town, they refused to turn the car around because of black cats, despite Mom's howling about the risk we were taking to ignore the black cat's warning. She would say, "Black cats are rare, and their warning is real. Something bad is going to happen, I know it."

Mom's grocery list was always small, consisting of essentials only. However, we could always tell when she had a little extra money. She would by a pack of real cigarettes instead of loose tobacco and rolling papers. We were always amazed to see the food in stores that other people ate. The most puzzling was milk in a paper box and chickens someone else killed. Unlike town kids, our days were not all spent in self-indulgent play. For instance, when blackberries and sand plums were in season, we got a bucket and did our part. There was nothing pleasant about wading through chiggers and ticks to harvest berries and plums. However, we knew there would be a reward of sweet, tangy jam and fruit butter at the end of our journey.

Certainly, the Duffy Place was the safest place in our world of uncertainty and chaos. Our father, ravaged by World War II, with persistent PTSD had become a prodigious alcoholic in an effort to turn off the war still raging in his mind. Back then, the term PTSD had not been coined. In fact, aviators who struggled with war memories were said to be "flack happy," which was tantamount to cowardice. What we saw was an angry and abusive drunk, who kept us in a constant state of fear frequently lashing out at us in anger as he flashed back to the war. Sadly, he was visited with uncontrollable and unpredictable emotions we could not understand, and he could not control or articulate.

# - 2 -
## THE BANTAM HEN

Mom always had an assortment of chickens. We would gather eggs every day and sacrifice a laying hen when we had no other meat. Sometimes, we had to endure a nasty peck from an old hen as we pushed under her to collect her warm egg. Mom had instructed us to leave the orange and grey Bantam hen alone to allow her to hatch her chicks. She said, "That bantam hen is a good mother. She always raises a good batch of chicks, so leave those eggs under her, even though none of them are hers. Bantams are feisty little hens that lay tiny eggs. Also, they are fast on their feet and can fly better than most chickens."

We watched the little hen closely, anticipating a playful batch of baby chicks to amuse ourselves with. However, when they hatched, we were appalled to find the hen had her own agenda, which did not include the meddling of three curious children. First, she raised her hackle feathers and postured to warn us off. That was enough for me, I was out of there. Red and Yvonne were not as easily discouraged and proceeded to try to catch one of the cute chicks they had isolated from the rest of the hatch. When they finally cornered the fuzzy little fellow, it began peeping frantically, which turned out to be an alarm call. Much to their surprise, the bantam hen could fly, and did so right into Red and Yvonne's faces. She clawed, pecked, and squawked as she ran them out of the chicken yard and collected her stray chick.

In addition to knowing everything, Yvonne was brave to a fault and would not be easily discouraged by a plucky little hen. She developed a plan, which of course, put Red and me at risk. Hiding behind the chicken coup, she waited for the right moment to dart out and collect a chick after we led the angry little hen far enough away to insure Yvonne was not in danger of being flogged. We understood our diversionary roll as she explained it.

"You go into the pin and get close to her chicks. When she chases you—"

I stopped her right there, "I don't want to do that."

She clarified that the mission was not voluntary, "You will do it or I will slap the spit right out of your face."

Having experienced that slap before, I decided the angry, little hen could not do worse. So, like good little soldiers, we set off—well actually, Red moved in and I walked in his shadow at a safe distance. Red darted into the hen's protective zone and she began to pursue us. At this point, I was in the lead. Yvonne darted out of the shadows and grabbed a chick, which immediately sounded its alarm call. The hen quickly diverted her attention from Red and covered the distance to Yvonne like a sprinter. Leaping into the air with wings flapping and feet flying, she began to claw and peck at Yvonne until she released the chick.

The mission was a failure. While Red and Yvonne fought over whose fault it was, I made a simple trap, patterned after the one Wile E. Coyote used to try to catch the Roadrunner. I placed a stick under the corner of a metal milk crate and sprinkled chicken scratch (a mixture of cracked corn and milo) under the crate, then waited with string in hand. Of course, every chicken but the right one pecked at the bait. Finally, the mean little critter took her turn at the feed and in fact, chased the other chickens away. I pulled the string—a clean catch! Red and Yvonne stopped throwing dirt, rocks, and curse words at each other when I approached them with not one but two fuzzy chicks. They promptly knocked me down and took the chicks away. I retaliated by releasing the little hen; after which I ran into the house to watch out the window as she chased them around the yard until they released her chicks. Predictably, they beat the crap out of me when they found my hiding place. However, it was worth it to have outsmarted them not once, but twice.

I stayed away from the two of them for the rest of the day. Playing by myself, I began putting together a matchbox tumblebug wagon train. Watching a tumble bug with a ball of cow manure, I realized they were exceptionally strong for their size. Tumblebugs scrape together a ball of fresh cow manure, ten times their size, after which they roll it to some spot they determine to be exactly right for laying a batch of eggs. Once the 'bug perfect' spot is located for the ball they've been rolling around for hours, they begin to dig under and around the prize until it is partially buried as a method of preserving the buried portion in a semisolid state. Finally, they push their eggs into the soft manure and set about finding another cow pile.

No question these tenacious insects have the stamina and strength to serve as fine mules for the matchbox wagon train. After gathering several tumblebugs into a pint mason jar, I cut lengths of string. Tying a knot, I secured the string to the empty matchbox by threading it through a small hole I bored into the box with a needle. With the harness attached, I retrieved a six-legged volunteer from the mason jar and attached her to the matchbox by tying the string at her abdomen. Predictably, the powerful girl began pulling the box across the floor. I started loading the wagon with plastic animals and marbles which did not seem to slow her gate. Truly, she made a fine mule. I repeated the process several times and had wagons moving all around me. To my dismay, each bug had its own sense of direction and instead of a train I had wagons marching off in every direction. Finally, I latched them all together. I expected them to move in a long train, one behind the other. Unfortunately, tumblebugs are territorial, and they began to fight, which entangled them and the wagons into a ball of wiggling bugs, boxes, and string. Red and Yvonne found me trying to untie the mules from my debunked wagon train. They pushed me away and took great joy in giving the wriggling mass several well placed stomps. Maybe a fitting end to *wagons hoe*…

# - 3 -
## MOM AND THE SWITCH

When, we were lucky enough to stay at the Duffy Place, we were tasked with gathering eggs and feeding the chickens. One fine day, for no reason at all—or maybe because we were just incorrigible little turd-hammers—we decided we would egg the chicken house. Mom caught us and cut a switch. Now, we knew with her limp she could not catch us, so we began running around the house as she chased us yelling, "You little turd-hammers! I'll teach you a lesson you won't forget. There will be no eggs for breakfast tomorrow!" We laughed and teased her by slowing down to taunt her. She was hopping mad by the time she finally wore out and stopped chasing us. We hid under the porch, one of our favorite hiding places, and plotted our next move.

We snuck to the back door, where we spied on her while she fixed lunch. We knew we were in for it when we saw the switch on the table. Mom was not a vengeful person, but when we really made her mad, she would make us stand for punishment before she would allow us to sit at her table. Fearing the inevitable, we acted like the smell of a cast-iron skillet full of chicken sizzling in lard, did not make our mouths water. In fact, we vowed we were not going to eat and give her the satisfaction of giving us the blistering we so richly deserved. Yvonne said, "I don't need her old fried chicken, do you?" With mouths watering, we lied and joined her in defiance. It was always better to agree with Yvonne.

After what felt like hours; most likely 10 minutes later, we relented and lined up for the switch first, followed by the best fried chicken on the planet. Predictively, she gave us her crooked little smile and a token switching. We ate with the gusto and haste of three little heathens ready for their next adventure. In fact, we always left the table at a dead run with food in our hands and pockets.

First order of business was to visit the newborn kittens in the hay barn. When we arrived at the location where their cagey mother hid them, we were greeted by a ghastly sight. Baby kitten carcasses were strewn over the haystack; they were partially eaten and covered with black flies. Fearing some hideous beast was hiding in the barn waiting to pounce on us, we fled screaming. When we got back to the house to tell Mom about the carnage, she gave us a taste of the switch once more for climbing on the haystack. Yvonne proclaimed defiantly, "It didn't hurt," and she got a second dose. I wailed like I was beaten half to death to be sure I would only feel the switch once. Red, true to form, to show Yvonne how tough he was, got a second dose for following her lead. After our punishments had been dealt, Mom smiled knowingly and explained to us that a tomcat had most likely killed the kittens because they were not his. She said, "That's just the way cats are. Now, get the shovel from the shed and bury them behind the pond—and be careful on that haystack."

We had a fine kitten funeral, at which we recited as many phrases as we could remember from Uncle Doyle's funeral. Afterward, we walked around talking tough and finally hatched an idea to kill the bad old tomcat. Certainly, we had not even considered how difficult it might be to kill a creature who was so elusive we had never actually seen him. Completely oblivious to reality, we planned to make spears by sharpening tree branches cut from the willows at the pond near the hay barn. We would need the corn knife, which we were forbidden to use, to cut and sharpen them. Yvonne ordered me to get the corn knife from the shed. After receiving a stern cursing for reminding her we were forbidden to use the corn knife, I argued back, "I don't want to get in trouble." Yvonne threatened, "Do you want me to snatch all the hair off your head?"

Knowing she did not make idle threats, I struck out for the tool shed. When I returned with the forbidden knife in hand, she reassured me we were quite justified in breaking the rules because the murderous tomcat had to die. Sticks in hand, we stomped around the barn driving our willow branch spears into hay bales to sharpen our Aboriginal spearing techniques, while we searched for the lair of the monster. Yvonne, sporting the forbidden corn knife through a loop of hay twine tied around her waist, barked orders like a drill sergeant. I am not quite sure how we did it but we actually located a wild cat in the back of the east hay loft. Knowing instinctively it was the murderous beast, we surrounded him and backed him into a corner. With hearts pounding and spears at the ready, we began advancing to impart the lethal blow.

The closer we got the more we realized how big the crouching creature really was. Finally, too close for comfort, the huge tomcat growled like a full-sized lion and lunged forward. That was all it took. We were out of there, running for our lives! Afraid he would get the last one down, we clambered down the ladder, all three of us at the same time. The corn knife lost in the hay, we ran for the house. When we got there, we told Mom about the beast and asked if we could borrow the gun to dispatch him. She offered us blackberry cobbler to get our mind off the cat and told us the gun was broken. Thankfully, that was the end of our quest to kill "Bad Tom."

In 1955 no one took swimming lessons, at least no one we knew. Convinced children were born with an innate ability to swim, dads armed with the wisdom of the ages and employing the justification, "That's how I learned to swim," simply flung their kids into the nearest pond. Not having the advantage of the daddy-sink-or-swim tutorial, we decided to teach ourselves to swim. Without question, Yvonne's determination and constant teasing and belittlement spurned us into action, and we headed for the small pond by the hay barn.

We waded out into the pond with the cool mud squishing between our toes and made our way to deep water. We had commandeered a metal gas can to use as a shared flotation device. Finally, the slimy bottom slipped away and we found ourselves clinging to the gas can handle and each other for dear life. Yvonne turned loose and disappeared underwater. Certain she had drowned, we began calling for her and kicking ourselves toward the nearest shoreline.

To our amazement and utter relief, she popped up next to the shore. Unbeknownst to us, she actually had the big-brother-sink-or-swim lesson and learned to swim underwater. When we kicked our way to her, she showed us the kicking and arm techniques that propelled her underwater. Careful to stay in shallow water we kicked along the cool, muddy bottom. Naturally, our swimming lesson quickly turned into a mud fight. We kicked along the bottom, scooped up mud, surfaced like urchin submarines, slung our mud, and ducked back under. Consequently, we spent the entire July afternoon in the pond and returned home with glaring sunburns. Fortunately, Mom had a tried and true sunburn cure: vinegar applied with a brown paper sack. The old home remedy was very soothing. We fell asleep, three ripe tomatoes, Olympic swimmers all, in a pile on the living room couch.

## - 4 -

# SOMETIMES YOU MUST RESORT TO SPITTING

In 1955 not many families had a TV. Coyote indulged himself with a black and white console model. He sat in front of it every evening and drank his pint of Old Crew (cheap, strong whiskey). In fact, he never dialed the TV unless it was time to watch Gorgeous George wrestle. He watched with his head resting in the greasy grey spot on the back of his recliner, which had developed over time from continued exposure to his unwashed hair. He would fall asleep from time to time and drool on the name tag of his blue work shirt, but he never loosened his grip on his Old Crew.

Let me say up front, we were not doting grandchildren. We ran wild with no adult supervision, and nothing was off limits. In fact, we took great sport in teasing Coyote and frequently continued our torment until he chased us. Giggling like we were playing tag, we would run and blast out of one of the three doors to the outside of the house, where we would get on our hands and knees in the dark and bay like coon hounds, which would elicit the comment from the Coyote, "Get the hell out of here, you damned dogs." The longest run was to the back door and only the bravest of the brave would make the long run.

One infamous evening, we had trouble motivating Coyote to vault from his chair and chase us a way like the wild little rats we were. Yvonne began by banging the back of his chair and calling him names. Keep in mind, this was her father she is abusing. On this night, he was in such a drunken stupor that she could not work him into enough of a rage to get him to play our game. She finally got in his face and called him 'Coyote'. It wasn't enough, so she leaned in and called him a son-of-a-bitch and spit in his face. That did it.

He came out of his chair like a missile, and the games were afoot. Red had chosen the long run, and in spite of the Yvonne's salivatory secretion stringing from his chin, Coyote keyed in on him and chased him like a mad bull. Red found out the hard way what none of us knew, Mom had hooked the latch on the screen door. He hit the door with a thud and a groan. Coyote slammed into him, knocking him through the screen and onto the back porch, where Coyote began kicking Red. He started to wail, fearing for his life, and rightfully so. Yvonne began calling Mom for help while she wrapped herself around Coyote's leg and bit him on the calf. He kicked her across the porch just as Mom arrived and began whacking him across the back and head with a broom. It took only a few whacks to drive him away, allowing Mom to do damage control.

Red and Yvonne were bleeding, I was crying, and Yvonne was cursing. She was trying to get the broom from Mom to go exact revenge on Coyote. He was already back in his chair taking a long pull of Old Crew, after which he smacked his lips twice and leaned back as if nothing had happened. Fortunately, the Coyote games were over. Mom tended to Red and Yvonne with a cool washcloth. Red's nose wasn't broken, and Yvonne's split lip would heal. We learned a valuable lesson—wait until the Old Crew has clawed its last and the bottle is empty before pursuing the Coyote. A staggering, drunk old fool is easier to outrun and outmaneuver than one who's only been lightly bitten by the Crow.

We awoke, as usual to the strong smell of coffee in the percolator, bacon frying, and Mom and Coyote arguing over money. We waited until Coyote, still in his work clothes from the day before, left for his job at the used car lot. We pulled on our respective glasses of whole cows' milk while Mom prepared eggs and bacon for breakfast. Yvonne pointed at Red's robust swollen nose and began to laugh and recount the Coyote Games. Red pointed to her busted lip, and they began to laugh together.

Mom, sober as a judge said, "You kids need to leave him alone. You may be playing, but he isn't. You're lucky you weren't hurt any worse." Things I will never forget... Coffee doesn't taste as good as it smells and neither does Old Crew. Milk on the other hand is a refreshing drink that tastes sweeter than cows smell.

**- 5 -**

## THE BIG PAYCHECK

Coyote had no marketable skills and no regular job. Rather, he went from job to job, living in the old family homes built in the 30's on land settled during the land run. The houses had been abandoned because their wood frames were detericrating, and with no insulation, they were difficult to heat with the old pot-bellied wood stoves. Coyote did not pay rent on a regular basis, but more or less lived at the behest, or more likely the sympathy, of the landowners.

One fine day Coyote, after receiving a handsome commission check for selling a used car, decided to celebrate with a trip to town. Bright and early the next morning, we were off to town in the Studebaker, where first thing, he secured a pint of Old Crew and began doing it up right. By 9:00 AM, he was staggering down the street in a drunken stupor flashing his money at everyone to show what a rich man he was. We walked along behind him watching the spectacle and acting like we didn't know him. With each passerby he would say, "What are you looking at? I got money. See here…" Then, he would reach into his pocket, drag out a wad of crumpled bills, and wave them in their face. Each time he pushed the money back into his pants, he would miss his pocket and put the money down his pants where it would work its way down his leg and fall onto the sidewalk. We happily retrieved each bill and placed them into Mom's eager hands. She would have grocery money, and we would not have to resort to a recon mission to get it.

Coyote passed out in the car and Mom, the worst driver in the world, had to drive us to the store, where she bought food and indulged herself with a book of crossword puzzles. While on our way home, struggling as white-knuckle driver Mom tolerated Yvonne's yelling and cursing as she drove. I think we held our breath the entire trip. At seven, Yvonne knew everything and was certain she could drive better than anyone, if only she had the chance, which fueled her frustration and anger at Mom's driving. Fortunately, Mom was able to keep the Studebaker between bar ditches and miss the culvert when she turned into the drive. She did, however, knock three boards off the end of the porch, and we counted our blessings.

After we helped Mom get the groceries inside, we snuck back to the car, where we tickled Coyote with grass to make him groan and scratch his face. Then, we dropped dried chicken droppings into his gaping mouth. I'll bet he had great breath the morning after. We are not sure when he dragged himself into the house, but he was in his bed still fully clothed the next morning. When he awoke, he quizzed Mom as to how he had spent his money. She smiled and replied, "You old fool, you spent it on Old Crew."

After breakfast we found the landowner cultivating the field behind the chicken house. We were intrigued by the process and sat on the old Gleaner combine, watching as he circled the field with a spring tooth in tow. Finally, Yvonne ran out and dove for the implement as it went by. Securing a hold on the outside corner spring, she was pulled in the soft soil, twisting and turning as she went. She teased us into trying it calling, "Don't be chicken. It's fun! Just try it." Red tried it and made sure he held on longer than she did, which prompted the Duffy descendant to yell, "You kids get the hell out of here! This isn't a toy." I was relieved I didn't have to take a turn as we took off at a dead run. Instead, we went to the large cage by the back door and teased the racoons who thought we were there to release them into the house, which certainly we would not do without Teddy's approval.

**- 6 -**

## THE RACCOONS AND OPOSSUM

Billy and Teddy crawled up in trees and dug into the ground to retrieve baby animals of all kinds. During the time we spent with them at the Duffy Place, they had a squirrel, an owl, two raccoons, a hawk, a bobcat, and a coyote. All of these critters either died or escaped from the huge cage outside the back door, except the two raccoons. Of all the wild animals they tried to make into pets, they had the most success with raccoons. Actually, there is something to the old saying, 'crazy as a pet coon'. The two raccoons were allowed to come in the house where they crawled all over the furniture, people, and everything in sight. Truly nothing was safe from their mischief.

I know cats hallucinate, and I suspect raccoons do too. Teddy would keep treats in his shirt pocket and the raccoons would run down the back of the divan and dive into his pocket with both hands. Now, if he sat down without a treat in his pocket, the raccoons would resort to biting him on the neck or the ear— and it was not an affectionate or playful bite. They would bring blood. Teddy's reaction was to slap them across the room, where they would spin around, growl at him, and run for a hiding place. Billy and Teddy finally realized the raccoons were too mean to be pets, and they released them into the wild.

Yvonne found a baby opossum, a stinky, slobbery little creature who was barely bright enough to feed itself. The opossum was named Baby O, and Yvonne lavished him with affection and even kissed the slobbery, stinky little thing. She kept it in a shoe box under her bed, and she got up in the night to feed it when it awoke. Billy and Teddy tried unsuccessfully to talk her out of keeping the grotesque little beast and finally resorted to stealing it one night. Yvonne confronted Teddy, and he admitted to destroying her Baby O. Yvonne lit into him like a wild cat, clawing and biting. He pushed her away, but it only made her madder. He finally locked his sister into a closet where she raved and beat on the door for hours.

After Teddy left the house, I made a huge mistake and let her out of the closet. She was mad that I had not liberated her sooner. After I returned to my play on the floor, she snuck up behind me and stabbed me in the back with a carpenter's pencil. I still have a souvenir of the incident in my back, a half inch piece of graphite. Red came to my rescue and began hammering Yvonne in the stomach with a continuous barrage of lefts and rights, driving her across the floor and back into the closet from which she came. Mom came with kerosene and medicated the hole in my back and covered it with a bandage. In those days, kerosene was the cure-all for every manner of cut, bruise, bump, or abrasion. After Teddy put several knots on Yvonne's head to get her attention, he asked her why she stabbed me. She told him, "I just wanted to see what it felt like to stab someone." Well, I can tell you from the receiving end, it's an unpleasant experience. Had it been anyone except Yvonne, I would have considered a reprisal of some kind. However, when you're dealing with the meanest creature on the planet, it's best to let sleeping dogs lie.

My back healed, and Yvonne never apologized, nor recounted the event. In fact, it was as if it never happened. I was happy to put it behind me and continue to be the third wheel in the mischief that graced our daily lives at the Duffy Place.

# THE OLD CROW

Coyote's nightly routine was to consume a pint of Old Crew while watching his TV. Without exception, he was never satisfied with one pint and would always search the car and barn looking for more whiskey. The Duffy Place had a porch that extended across the back of the house. The boards were rough, untreated lumber and were literally rotting to the ground. His nightly routine included a trip out back where he finished off his pint and tossed the empty bottle under the porch through a hole where the boards had rotted away. Then after urinating and passing gas, he would stagger away and end up passed out on his bed.

We found the rotting old porch to be a safe haven and a quick hide away when we were playing Poke the Coyote. Finding our hideaway strewn with Old Crew bottles and knowing the importance of a bottle of whiskey to an alcoholic, we hatched an idea. We began pouring the leavings from each bottle together to create a full bottle. Our intent was to extort money from the Coyote when he became desperate for a drink. When we began our undertaking, there were several bottles already under the porch, and we quickly had a half bottle of the pale-yellow liquid. Impatiently waiting for more discards, we began talking about how we would spend the money. Of course, Yvonne would be the one who actually perpetrated the extortion, and we would be going along for the ride. Yvonne was convinced that we could hold the old fool up for ten dollars, of which she would take half for brokering the deal. Certainly, five dollars was more money than we had ever seen, so we were more than okay with the arrangement.

After what seemed like a month, our ten-dollar bottle of whiskey was still only two thirds full, and we were out of patience. Suddenly, Red had a flash of intuition. He realized that we could finish off the pint with just any yellow liquid and the strong flavor of the cheap whiskey would mask the taste. Now, we could easily write our names in the snow with urine, so it was no task for us to direct the stream into the slender neck of the Old Crew bottle—and that was exactly what we did. As it turned out, the task was not as easy as we thought because we were unsteady with our aim as we snickered uncontrollably.

A few days later, a night of desperation for Coyote finally came. One Saturday evening after drinking all day, Coyote was out of whiskey and began the car and barn search. I scurried under the porch and retrieved our pale-yellow treasure, and fearlessly Yvonne began the extortion. Once Coyote realized that he could not threaten her into surrendering the prize, he began to negotiate. He started at the Liquor Store price of four dollars. He received a stern response of "Hell, no!" until he finally surrendered a ten-dollar bill. Of course, he tried to kick Yvonne as she snatched it from his hand and ran from the house laughing loudly.

Naturally, we had to watch his reaction as he drank the urine-laced whiskey. So we snuck back into the house and peeked around the corner from the kitchen. We held our collective breaths as he took the first pull from the bottle. Amazed that he did not react to the taste of urine, we begin to snicker. The mean old bastard was drinking our pee and liking it. The snicker quickly escalated into laughing out loud. His response was to ask us 'dammed kids' what was so funny, which made us laugh even louder. Mom came in to see what was up, and after we told her, she began laughing with us. Our laughter reached a crescendo each time he took a pull from the Old Crew bottle and continued until it was empty. Without question, this was one of the best evenings we spent at the Duffy Place.

Unfortunately, the five dollars never reached our hands. However, we got to share candy and pop and revel in our victory over Coyote. We did get the last laugh after all because Yvonne was still envious of our ability to write our names in the snow and shoot urine far out into the pond.

# THANKSGIVING HOLIDAY AT GRANDMAS

My father's family did not get together often because of their tendency to drink too much and become violent. However, one Thanksgiving we found ourselves on the way to, what turned out to be, a very volatile family reunion. My father started drinking early the morning of the auspicious occasion and provided us with a wild ride during which he hit my mother several times for telling him to slow down. By the time we arrived we were afraid to speak or be seen because of the scary and violent ride. Certainly, had we not been stuck in the car, we would have found a safe hiding place. In fact, we ran from the car when we arrived and found a bed to hide under.

My Aunt Lucille was there, she and my father began arguing almost instantly. As I recall, she called him a drunk, and he called her a bitch and told her to mind her own business. My mother went to the bathroom to clean the blood off her face and to determine where we were hiding. When she found us under a bed, she lay on the floor and told us everything was okay despite the escalating argument and promise of violence in the next room. She coaxed us out of hiding, and we found a table of food and desserts in the dining room. Also to our amazement, we found our sweet-hearted Aunt Leana sitting by herself in the living room.

Why she married into this family I will never know. My mother scooted us up next to her and went into the kitchen to see if she could intercede and maybe salvage some of the day. Unfortunately, as she walked through the door the argument got violent. My father struck his sister, and she grabbed his arm and bit the soft part of his hand, opening an ugly wound. After he knocked her down, my uncle grabbed my father and shoved him out the door, telling him to cool off.

The wrinkled, mean old woman (my grandmother) charged through the broken screen door and ordered my father to get off her property, abruptly ending the Thanksgiving celebration. I am sure our entire visit lasted less than thirty minutes. My mother drove us home while my father sprinkled salt into the wound on his hand and made vulgar remarks about his sister.

My father was a crack shot and always had a gun with him. In this case it turned out to be handy because doves resting on the electrical lines made easy targets. My mother was well schooled in the proper driving methods for harvesting the unsuspecting critters. She would put the car in neutral and allow it to roll to a stop, at which point the twenty-two rifle would crack, and the dove would fall to the ground. Ah yes, Thanksgiving dinner.

As it turned out, my father quit drinking. He took pride in his shooting and was actually laughing and having a good time as we scrambled to the fluttering birds and retrieved them like good little bird dogs. When we got home, my mother breasted the doves and began cooking them. Our hunger was so great that the dove breast, along with bread and gravy, seemed to us better than turkey and dressing. And not having a violent evening was certainly better than dessert. My brother and I actually fell asleep in our shared bed instead of under it.

When mother woke us the next morning with a smile, we eagerly dressed in anticipation of more pleasant family time. Unfortunately, my father was hungover and suffering from withdrawal. My mother shushed us and told us that he had a headache and we needed to be quiet. Later, when he ordered her to return home on her break with a bottle of whiskey, we knew it was starting over and our appetite quickly disappeared.

The unfortunate truth is, alcoholics are never on an even keel. They're either drunk, hungover, or suffering from withdrawal. Each condition brings its own personality-altering consequences. Each are equally unpleasant, but different. On this particular morning following Thanksgiving, he had no patience for his children and drove us from the room calling us 'irritating little bastards'. We slipped under the bed and hoped he wouldn't decide to pick on us to amuse himself.

# - 9 -
## THE BIG POND

Mom would take us fishing at the big pond. The pond was one-half mile from the Duffy house. It was a muddy pond with holes pushed into the mud by cattle walking out to water and cool themselves on hot summer days. We walked in our pecking order on the way to the pond. Yvonne as always, was in the lead, with Red in tow and I would be third. Mom would bring up the rear with Carlene, holding her hand. Mom had a fine carry-all fishing seat also known as a five-gallon bucket. The possible items in her bucket included Garrett's snuff, Camel cigarettes, fried chicken, water, and catfish bait. Chicken liver was her bait of choice. My uncles Billy and Teddy would appear later to tease us and show off in the water. These scrapping boys were larger than life, in my estimation giant hulks of men. In reality, they were barely 5' 7", tan, lean, muscled, and tough as nails with fighting skills they honed by prowling the local pubs looking for trouble and scrapping with each other at the drop of a hat.

Mom's cane pole was configured with 15 foot of string. The casting method was interesting. It started with the line in hand, followed by pushing the pole away from you while you simultaneously lifted the tip and released the line in one continuous motion. The cork, stink bait and all, would settle gently onto the water, barely making a splash. Mom had the motion down pat and her bobber would land far out into the pond. She would make us stay out of the water so she could catch fish for supper—certainly, a situation we did not relish. In fact, we gave her no peace and pleaded to go in the water constantly with Yvonne cursing her and calling her names. Interestingly, when Mom finally relented, telling us, "You little turd-hammers go ahead and make a dammed mess of the water," she began catching fish. She lit up a cigarette to celebrate and became amused with our antics in the mud. The fish must have been stimulated by our splashing because she was building quite a nice stringer of slimy green mud cats.

My baby sister Carlene watched us swim under water and decided she could do the same. She leaned over in the shallow water and stuck her head under and began walking forward like an old turkey searching for corn. Unfortunately, she did not understand that you had to hold your breath while you were under water. She took a long-wet breath of muddy water, jerked her head out of the water, cried "Mom," fell over backwards, and went back under. Yvonne rescued her and began to laugh and make fun of her, and we followed suit. Mom said, "You kids get the hell out of here!" And she pulled scared, crying, muddy, snotty-nosed Carlene to the carry-all fishing seat and began to console her and clean her up.

Red, running from the mud fight, disappeared in a deep hole that none of us knew existed. Teddy appeared to be bouncing on springs as he bounded across the water along the edge of the pond, to rescue Red. Red popped up and gurgled, "Help," and disappeared in the muddy water, just as Teddy reached the deep hole. Without hesitation, Teddy jumped in after him. Teddy came up with Red, who was squirming and spewing muddy water. Red was almost as tough as Yvonne. As soon as he could draw a full breath, he said, "I can swim under water, you know. I was swimming my way along the bottom to shallow water. I really didn't need help." Teddy slapped him on the back of the head and walked away.

Teddy stopped in his tracks with a loud, "Shit! I lost my billfold with twenty dollars in it." We looked for hours to no avail. Twenty dollars was a lot of money in 1955. Finally, with long willow tree shadows cast across the pond, it was time to make the lengthy, arduous half-mile trip back. Now, the carry-all fishing seat was quickly converted into a redneck creel with eight wriggling catfish in the bottom. Mom carefully dipped it into the pond to allow water to spill over the rim and into the bucket. Once the backs of the wriggling green and yellow cats were covered, she handed the handy-dandy creel to Yvonne and admonished her not to spill any. After only a few yards, Red was next, and he carried that bucket of green wriggling slime the rest of the way home, just to remind us he was stronger than we were and to prove he was undaunted by his near drowning.

Physically the trip to the big pond was difficult for Mom. She had a torn tendon on her right knee, causing it to give way if she extended it too far. Her injury was caused by an eighteen-hundred-pound work horse stepping on her barefoot in the mud. The incident stripped most of the skin and tissue off her foot along with her toenails; one of which, grew back thick and black like a horse's hoof. Her knee was injured at the same time. She quite literally tore the tendon loose from her knee, trying in desperation to wrench herself free while the horse's hoof slid slowly from her instep to the tip of her toes, stripping off tissue as it went.

She also had a bladder problem, most likely from the problematic birth of one of her five children. Without question, she was the poster child for frequent urination. She would stop four or five times on the half-mile trek to the pond, saying "You kids go on now, I need to pee." Without the encumbrance of underwear, she was quick and efficient at draining her miniscule bladder. She raised her dress away from her body, slightly cock her bad leg out in a funny manner and turned loose with a cup or so of urine. Needless to say, she always had a strong smell of urine about her, but she was so sweet to us, we weren't the least bit put off by her persistent outhouse odor.

Back in Mom's kitchen she got busy with her fish skinning pliers and a butcher knife. The process was nothing, if not gruesome. First, she had to poleax the squirmy critters with a sixteen-penny nail driven through their heads and into the porch. Next, she cut a ring around their head and stripped their skin off. Finally, with the finesse of a brain surgeon she sliced the belly open and removed the entrails without cutting into them. Washed with well water, cut into chunks and floured, they were ready for the skillet. Old timers will tell you the way to eat mud catfish is to bake them on a cedar board until they're well done, then throw the fish in the trash and eat the board. Mud cats taste exactly like the mud they live in. However, if we wanted to eat another meal at Mom's table, we had better rave about how good they were and eat them with a smile because she was more than proud of her accomplishment. We piled up on the couch and fell asleep in the living room, grimy little urchins still wearing the mud from the day's adventure. Consumed by the blissful ignorance of youth, we thought nothing of witnessing two near-drownings and a harrowing rescue.

# 10

# THE COON HUNT

My two Uncles Billy and Teddy had several skinny Coon Hounds that lay around the yard and under the porch. The only thing I ever saw them do was run the chickens out of their dust wallows under the big cedar trees and dig them deep enough to reach damp cool soil for themselves. And that's where they spent their long, hot summer days. You couldn't tell by their look or demeanor, but these dogs were crackerjack coon hounds. In fact, they were some of the best hounds in the county with hunting skills honed during frequent-all night hunting trips.

On what seemed to be a particularly dark night, we were invited to accompany the coon hunting duo on one of their forays into the darkness to pursue the masked enemy. Teddy lowered the tailgate on the rusty green Studebaker truck and whooped the dogs into the truck with a long "Woooooo," which instantly set the dogs to baying as they clambered into the back of the Studebaker, with the three of us—my brother Red, Yvonne, and I—right behind them. We made our way to the front of the truck through the maze of eagerly wagging, leg-whopping hound dog tails. The hounds stuck their heads out the side of the truck, their ears and lips flapping in the wind with slobbers coating the side rail of the truck. The three of us stood up behind the cab collecting bugs on the teeth we exposed with smiles of joyful anticipation of the ensuing adventure. Red and I were particularly elated to be on this hunt because our mother was able to get away from our nightmare to spend some time with us at the Duffy Place, and she came along.

We arrived at a location known to be full of the ring-tailed critters we sought, and as soon as the truck rolled to a stop the dogs boiled out the back and off the sides of the truck and bolted into the woods. We sat on the rusty tailgate listening in the dark as Billy and Teddy told tales of previous coon hunts. They kept an ear out for the dogs baying in the dark woods and periodically Teddy would stop talking and say things like, "I think Old Blue just struck." It was as if the dogs were talking to him. He knew each dog by its voice and could tell by the intensity and frequency of their baying when the dogs struck a fresh trail, when they had a racoon treed, and when they had one in water. A raccoon in the water is particularly dangerous to dogs because, as we heard in one of the tailgate stories, they can outswim a dog. And when a dog is completely spent, a racoon will ride on his head and drown him.

Billy and Teddy also knew every terrain feature in the area and would say things like, "They are in the slue below the burr oak tree." Sometimes the dogs would chase deer, and Billy and Teddy could tell by the path they took, the change in their voice, and their speed of travel. Teddy would say, "Damn, they're on a deer again." The dogs gave up their deer trails quickly because the deer quickly out-distanced them and the trails grew cold. In fact, it wasn't long before the dogs struck a raccoon trail and the hunt was on again.

As the dogs began to close in on a raccoon their baying became more intense which signaled the time to begin the trek through the dark woods to find them at the base of a tree where the raccoon had taken refuge. Teddy said, "They've got him!" And off we went with only two flashlights between us. Of course, the pecking order was maintained; consequently, I was bringing up the rear in the dark about to pee myself. Billy and Teddy moved so quickly through the woods, even Yvonne had trouble keeping up. Teddy shined the light back to check on the procession, and realizing I was scared speechless hoisted me to his shoulders with a reassuring, "Come on Froggy, I'll get you there." I felt on top of the world… plus, the afraid-of-the-dark lump in my throat went away. With tree limbs and leaves scraping my face, we moved quickly through the thick woods. It seemed like we had traveled for miles as our excitement and the intensity of the baying dogs increased.

When we arrived we found the dogs circling a huge oak tree, baying and fighting among themselves, as they sniffed and reared up on the tree. Billy shined his light into the tree and there he was, the masked bandit, with bright yellow eyes staring defiantly down at us. I wondered who would climb the tree and shake him out. Fortunately, Teddy knew what to do. He used a "squalling" technique to inspire the raccoon to jump to the ground. He began making a high-pitched squalling sound by pinching and shaking his cheek while making an eerie high-pitched growling sound. Remarkably, the confused raccoon became more and more agitated and finally jumped from the tree into the middle of six dogs, where he was instantly mauled to death. The fight only lasted a few seconds. For me, the intensity and noise of the fight was terrifying and exciting at the same time. Standing on the ground, flashlight in hand, it occurred to me that the raccoon might run up my pant leg to escape the carnage. I began backing away and finally stumbled over backwards with the flashlight shining on my face. My uncles had a good laugh at my expense. Billy said, "What's wrong, Froggy? That old raccoon is dead as a hammer." as he hoisted me to my feet and dusted me off.

I puzzled over the raccoons behavior for years. What could have possessed that critter to cause him to jump from the safety of the tree into a wad of dogs, flashlights, and people? As I replayed the incident in my mind, I realized the raccoon made the same squalling noise during the forty-five seconds he fought for his life as Teddy made when he "squalled" him from the tree. The smart little critter must have thought the dogs were occupied fighting another raccoon, and he had a chance to slip away unscathed. At any rate, when the dogs quit shaking and tossing him around Billy collected the lifeless broken body to be skinned, dried, and sold later for fifty cents.

Teddy gathered me up and hoisted me to his shoulders with a "Let's go home, Froggy," and we struck out for the Studebaker. Of course, most of us had no clue which way to go; however, Teddy knew exactly where we were and guided us on the shortest route back to the truck. We were crossing an open field talking and laughing about the successful hunt when suddenly Teddy said, "Quiet!" In the silence we could hear a thundering noise, which the flashlight revealed to be a herd of Brahma cattle. Teddy exclaimed, "They're Brahmas! Run!" Luckily, all I had to do was hold on to Teddy's head while we ran for our lives. Fortunately, Teddy was a kind and patient man and didn't lose his temper when he had to admonish me twice not to cover his eyes as, with the resolve of a scared five-year-old, I clung to him for dear life. At the fence Teddy swung me around his shoulder and to the ground safely on the other side. He waited for Red and Yvonne and slung them over the fence when they arrived. Billy placed one hand on the fence post and swung over the fence and around, landing with his body facing the agitated heard of cattle. He helped Teddy get my mother through the fence while yelling and waving at our pursuers. Teddy was last to vault over the fence. We were safe. Suddenly, it was funny to shine our flashlights into their blue-green eyes and pummel them with rocks. Teddy whooped the dogs back into the Studebaker. The three of us piled up on Billy, Teddy, and my mother in the front

of the Studebaker and fell asleep as we returned to the lair of the
Coyote.

# 11

# THE RECON MISSION

My grandfather's name was Ted, though we called him Coyote, the name his son Teddy gave him. Coyote had a full head of white hair, he was about 5'6" tall, with bad teeth stacked side-by-side along his bottom jaw, giving him a particularly vicious look—and vicious he was. We watched from the hay loft as he kicked a three-day old calf to death while trying to break it from its nursing mother to drinking from a bucket. Without question, he lived up to his name in many ways. He was a mean, hateful, difficult, and selfish man who neither nurtured, provided for, or even cared about the welfare of his children.

As an alcoholic, he could not hold down a steady job and seldom worked at all. However, when he did manage to put a few dollars in his pocket, true to form, he refused to share the money with Mom to allow her to buy food for the household. At night after he drank himself into a stupor and passed out on the bed, Mom would send us in to retrieve money from his pockets. It was easier when he took his pants off and hung them on the bed post; but if necessary, we would reach into his pockets to retrieve the money while he snored and spewed vial smelling alcohol breath.

As children we were blissfully detached from the sadness of the situation and foolishly considered it a great adventure. Actually, I shouldn't say 'we' because Yvonne did the actual pilfering and we were along for the ride, basically to make us feel like we had contributed in some way. There we were, thieves in the night, trying not to giggle as we low-crawled across the cool wood floor on our mission of thievery. Foolish, because he would have tried to kill us if he had caught us in the act. Yvonne would reach into his pockets, careful not to jingle his belt buckle or the loose change in his pocket. She would hand the money to Red, and Red in turn handed the bills to me. As you might imagine, I felt really important as I handed the money to Mom.

Another recon mission we were tasked with was keeping the snipe jar full. Both Coyote and Mom were heavy tobacco users. Their preference was camel cigarettes; however, when money was scarce, which was most of the time, Mom would resort to smoking tobacco from snipes, cigarette butts, with a little tobacco and a lot of tar left near the filter after they were discarded. She would field strip them and put the remaining dab of tobacco into a pipe and smoke it. In fact, we would pick snipes up off the streets and put them in our pockets to be added to the emergency tobacco stash in the snipe jar. Occasionally, she would resort to Garret's Snuff when she was desperate to feed her habit. Another of our missions was to make sure Coyote's last cigarette didn't burn up in the ashtray when he passed out.

## - 12 -
## THE TURTLE HUNT

The Duffy Place was near Black Bear Creek, named such because in the thirties there were black bears in Oklahoma, and rumor had it that there were still a few bears left in 1955. Mom loved to fish and would take any opportunity to do so. Black Bear Creek was one of her favorite spots, but we had to drive to it, and remember she was the worst driver in the world.

One spring Billy and Teddy visited a particular sand bar on the Black Bear where the soft-shelled turtles nested. Mom reminded them every day that the full moon was coming on Friday, and it would be time to dig for nesting turtles and their eggs. Friday morning, Teddy asked me in front of everyone, "Froggy, are you ready to dig for softies today?" With that, we all sprang into action. Mom got her twelve-foot cane pole, fishing bucket, and a box of frozen shrimp. Red, Yvonne, and I put on our bathing suits and grabbed towels and a blanket for lying in the sun on the sand bar.

We loaded into the Studebaker pickup, Billy, Teddy, and Mom in front. The rest of us piled into the back with a couple of coon hounds. The Black Bear wasn't far away, and we were there before we knew it. The sand bar was in the middle of the creek.

Billy and Teddy headed straight for it with buckets, shovels, and gunny sacks in hand. Mom found a shady spot on the muddy bank where she pushed her bucket into the soft mud and set about threading the stinky shrimp onto her hook. Red, Yvonne, and I waded out, until we had to resort to swimming, with our towels and blanket held high overhead to get through the deep water between the sand bar and the shore. Mom wasted no time getting her line in the water with the stinky shrimp suspended below a real cork float.

By the time the three of us arrived at the sand bar, Teddy had already located and captured a soft-shelled turtle. It was a small one about the size of a dinner plate. He held it up for us to see. It had webbed feet tipped with sharp claws, a long thin neck that ended with a snorkel-like nose no bigger than a drinking straw, with an overall shape like that of a Frisbee. Mom shouted from the shore, "That's just the right size for frying!"

We went to the end of the sand bar where it tailed out downstream to swim. The Bear was a deep, lazy creek with slow-moving water. The current moved gently past us, carrying cotton from the cottonwood trees, as part of their annual effort to propagate. Alligator gar glided along in the meandering creek, rising to the surface, wheezing and popping their bony-toothed snouts as they gulped air from the surface. We were afraid of them of course, because they had the word 'alligator' in their name.

Billy and Teddy had located a really big softy and were digging frantically to catch her before she dug deeper in the sand to escape. Billy shouted, "You kids come and get these eggs. We ran to the sight of the hunt and began picking up the leathery cherry-sized eggs as they rose out of the sandy water. Teddy finally dived into the hole and shouted "Got him!" as he pulled out a huge platter with squirming legs. We grabbed the gunny sack to help and ran for the turtle. Red got too close and received a nasty bite. It didn't break the skin, but he had a magnificent bruise for a week or so, a battle scar he wore proudly.

Mom yelled "Got him!" as she pulled a huge squirming channel cat out of the water. It went in her gunny sack and quickly back into the water. We just had to swim over to look at the whiskered bruiser, and we received a scolding as little turd-hammers who had messed up her fishing by swimming right through her fishing hole. We jumped back in the water laughing and made our way back to the sand bar.

As the day lingered slowly by, Mom caught several more catfish, and Billy and Teddy filled their sack with softies. The quiet and peaceful day unfortunately had to end, and we tumbled our sunburned sandy bodies into bed without a bath and fell instantly to sleep, grit and all.

Sometime in the night, I am guessing around midnight, we were awakened by an angry voice, "Where are my damned kids?" In minutes we were huddled in the back seat of the Mercury on our way back to the nightmare. To this day, I have no idea how fresh fried soft-shell turtle, or their eggs, taste. We never spoke of our disappointment, or of anything we did while we were at the Duffy Place. We knew if we did, our father, uncertain of himself and everything around him, would not allow us to go back.

# THE SHRIVELED OLD WOMAN

One day we left the safety of the Duffy Place, loading up in the old green Mercury to visit the meanest troll on the planet, our father's mother. Being a recent immigrant from Austria, she spoke broken English when she tried to communicate with us. However, she cursed us in German when she was unhappy with us, which was more often than not. We were told she immigrated from Austria with our grandfather, who we had never seen. We didn't call her grandmother or grandma or anything at all because we were afraid to speak in her presence or look her in the eye. She lived alone. Rumor has it, she drove my grandfather away with a gun and reported him deceased to get title to the property. For some reason Red and I were left in her care, and it was nothing like being left at the Duffy Place with Mom. She made us work constantly, pulling weeds in the garden and hauling water. She was mean as a snake, never spoke an encouraging word to us, and was never satisfied with our work.

She had an open well and a strange bucket; it was nothing more than a thin pipe with a trap door in the bottom. The trap door in the bottom was actuated by the weight of the pipe, which would allow water to flow in. The trick was not to let it go too far down in the water or risk filling it with so much water it could not be pulled out. Of course, while trying to make the old woman happy, Red and I did the wrong thing. We lowered the bucket so far into the well we could not get it out. The old woman found us struggling to get it free and threatened us with, "You either get my bucket out of that well, or I will throw you two down there with it." Having no reason to doubt the hateful old hag, we redoubled our efforts. Wrapping the rope around our frail little arms, we pulled for all we were worth. Finally, rope burned and bleeding, it came to the top and we triggered the water release, saving us from a watery grave.

We were ordered into bed as soon as we had eaten and were admonished to remain quiet and not leave our room until morning. Strangely, the blue ceiling of the bedroom had black cat tracks across it. We were afraid to ask but assumed the mean old woman had scared the cat so badly that he walked upside down on the ceiling to get away from her. In the night I had to pee, so Red and I snuck out of the room and headed to the back door. We were greeted by a ghastly sight—the mean old woman was returning from a trip to the outhouse, and she was completely naked. Her body was grey with sagging wrinkles and bulging blue veins from head to toe. She lit into us, raving like a mad woman driving us back to our room. And guess what, a ghastly sight will suck the pee right out of your bladder.

Mid-week, we got a reprieve when my aunt and uncle from down the road showed up to visit us and took us to their house for a meal and an overnight stay. We were amazed they actually showed an interest in us. They spoke to us kindly, and my aunt made cookies and gave us a warm hug before bed. We thought we had died and gone to heaven and believed we were going to get to stay with them instead of Brunhilda. Unfortunately, the very next day the witch arrived to retrieve us back to the labor camp. We cried and clung to my aunt, and she shed tears with us. However, the old hag got her way and the fairytale was over.

With square shovels in hand, she dragged us to her stinky, dusty chicken coup. She ordered us to clean it out by dark if we wanted to eat. We knew no matter what we did, it wouldn't be enough to suit her. Trying hard to please so she would feed us at the end of the day, we scraped deep in the ground where we uncovered five one-pint mason jars of opossum grape wine buried in the back corner. I am sure my grandfather made it and hid it from the mean, old witch. We opened the mason jars and drank the thick beverage, grape skins and all. We were five and six, and it didn't take much for us to get drunk. Then strangely, our fear of the old woman disappeared and we began to play a game of hide and seek with her. In fact, we hid from her the whole day, which worked out in our favor because we were ordered off her property.

Fearing we had run away, she contacted our parents, informing them we were missing. When they arrived we came out of hiding and ran to the car. We happily took a beating, after which we were loaded into the car and taken back home. We found out years later that during our absence our father had gone on a failed job interview. True to form, he took his disappointment out on my mother which prompted her to return us to the Duffy Place, the safe place, where we spent our best days.

# - 14 -
# A SAFE PLACE

I wondered for years why we spent so much time with my grandmother (Mom). I now realize that even with the rickety old house, the drunken Coyote, and the meanest person in the world Yvonne, it was still the safest place we could be. Mother would sneak away from the nightmare she lived and visit us when she could.

Sometimes, she would think the nightmare was over, and she would come to take us home. Unfortunately, nothing ever changed on the home front, and she had actually brought us back into harm's way. Our father was a war hero who came back from World War II to small town America with no skills and no education, the sum of which equated to no opportunity—at least no opportunity he considered to be up to par for a war hero. Having been decorated with two silver stars, two bronze stars, and two oak leaf clusters, he truly was a war hero. Unfortunately, we as a nation, in our haste to forget the ravages of war, tended to forget our heroes who couldn't walk away from it so easily.

My poor mother watched his life deteriorate from that of a proud man with a history of bravery and distinguished service, to an angry alcoholic, unsure of himself and everyone around him.

His nightly routine was to self-medicate his feelings of guilt, anger, and inadequacy with strong drink. I'm not sure of his choice of poison, but I am sure it was no better than the Old Crew his father in-law consumed. Unfortunately, he was an angry and violent drunk who vented his anger first on his wife, and then his children. Many a time my mother would step between us and the angry drunk, taking a beating that was intended for us. I will never outgrow the guilt I felt as I listened from under the bed to Mother taking a beating to protect me. We were not bad kids. We never knew what might set him off. Therefore, we quickly learned the best thing to do when the raving started was to hide.

One particularly bad night, Mother was a few minutes late from her waitressing job. He confronted her at the door, accusing her of a clandestine meeting with some rich bastard she met at the cafe. She showed him the sack of groceries and explained that we were out of milk and bread. He slapped her with the back of his hand, knocking her down and breaking the glass bottles of milk. Trying not to cry, because it infuriated him, she swore nothing was going on and begged him not to hit her again. He ordered her to clean up the mess. And to drive home his point, he grabbed her by the hair on the back of her head, jerked her violently against his body, leaned down to her 5' 4" height, and in a hissing whisper, he said, "You do know I will kill you and skin these two little bastards if I catch you cheating."

Shaking the strands of hair from his hand, he turned and looked at my brother and me, which sent us flying out of the room and under the bed. As the night went on, his rage only grew worse. The meal was not good enough, so he threw the plate across the room and into the wall adjacent to our hiding place. We shuttered and shed silent tears as we heard the abuse of our mother escalate. Trust me, when you fear for your life, you can weep in silence. The beating continued as usual until he passed out, despite my mother begging repeatedly for him to stop as she swore there was no one in her life but him.

Finally, it got quiet and Mother came and sat on the floor beside the bed and encouraged us to come out. We were so happy to see her alive, we wept as she hugged and reassured us that she was okay. To this day the smell of her blood resonates in my brain, waking me in the night when, until I get my bearings, I'm a frightened five-year-old boy afraid of the dark, reaching for his mother. She always blamed the war and his bad memories for his violent behavior. I think she truly believed he suffered from what we now know to be post-traumatic stress disorder. Back then they called it 'shell shock' and, considered a sign of weakness, no one talked about it and no one got help.

Without exception, the morning after, he would cry and apologize and blame his violence on bad war memories. This time, he offered a kind of apology by way of blaming his bad emotions on the memories of Garrett's (my namesake) violent death at the hands of a German patrol that pursued them after their B-17 was shot down behind enemy lines. My mother would always forgive him and cry with him as he swore it would never happen again. Covering her bruises with makeup, she would tell us to be good and remind us not to talk about what happens to anyone. She always warned us that if someone found out, the government would take us away from her and put us in a boys home.

Most nights, we would huddle outside the house, watching and listening to the raging of a chemically insane man. Mother knew just when to escape. She would time it to where he was too drunk to pursue us, but not drunk enough to be violent. She would calmly gather us up into a soft blanket, shushing us so we could escape undetected. We would go to sleep in the safety of her arms huddled outside in a dark corner and awake in our shared bed the next morning. The night I remember most was not because of violent behavior, but because we had been given some purple pills to treat a pinworm infection which caused us to have purple diarrhea throughout the night, which reeked of a strong chemical smell.

The sad thing was that we thought all kids lived this way. Red and I have never talked about the beatings, or the fear and guilt we felt. And trust me, we took our share of beatings, and we felt guilty every time we hid while our mother took a beating. To this day, we do not discuss the horrors of our childhood. It is as if we can keep them locked away as if they are merely a bad dream if we just don't speak of them out loud.

On her way to work the morning after a violent night, Mother would take us back to the Duffy Place where she would leave us with her mother (Mom), along with Yvonne and her brothers, Billy and Teddy. Billy would always walk her back to the car and encourage her to stay or to run away. Unfortunately, she knew she had to return to her nightmare or put her entire family in harm's way. She considered running away, but where would she go? And how would she live? She was twenty years old with three children and no education. So, she returned to her nightmare hoping against hope that she could help him come out of it and find a way to live a normal life, knowing full well his promises were hollow—well-intentioned, but hollow. However, she found solace in the fact that her children were in a safe place when she left us with Mom for days on end.

# – 15 –
# THE CAR WRECK

My father's nightly routine was to drink until he passed out. Unfortunately, before he reached the point in which his flashbacks ended, he would find an excuse to abuse my mother and the two of us if we weren't smart enough to go into hiding. Since we never knew what would set him off, we played quietly and kept our wits about us. With his exemplary war record he had no problem finding work. Unfortunately, because of what was perceived to be a cavalier attitude about showing up for work, he was unable to keep a job for long; therefore, we moved around pursuing one job after another.

We loaded our possessions into the green Mercury and left Texas bound for Wichita, Kansas, where he was promised a job at Boeing. With no money for an overnight stay, we were attempting to drive straight through. My mother was driving, Red was asleep in the back seat, and I was laying in the back-window gazing at stars. Suddenly my mother shouted, "Oh no!" She stood on the brakes and swerved to the right. I rolled on my side just in time to see a Collie dog fighting with another dog in the middle of the road. The car was instantly out of control on the curve, slid off the pavement, and rolled down a steep embankment. We were all tossed about and battered. Additionally, Red and I were battered repeatedly by the mantel clock that was in the back window with me. I lost consciousness, but regained it in the emergency room of a local hospital, staring at the ceiling. Red was cut and bleeding, as were my mother and father. Fortunately, all I had was a bloody nose and a swollen eye, which later turned black.

For as long as I can remember, my mother made sure Christmas was special for everyone she loved. She would buy and hide things throughout the year. She called it 'squirreling them away'. The car accident occurred on Christmas Eve. Consequently we spent Christmas Day bruised and battered in a flea bag motel. Determined to make Christmas special. My mother unable to chop down a small cedar tree in a nearby pasture downed it with two shots from a twelve-gauge shotgun. Propping it up in a corner of the room she decorated it with meager findings from a convenience store. Finally, she retrieved our gifts from the car trunk and wrapped them in bright shiny paper. My mother always spoke of that Christmas as the best ever. Because she was inspired and relieved beyond measure by my reaction to her efforts to make Christmas special in that broken-down motel. She said I squatted down in front of the tree with two glaring black eyes, next to Red with stitches in his lip, and smiling from ear to ear, I declared the packages to be "toys, all toys". My mother's life was never easy. However, she received the blessings of hope and faith year after year as she relived that special Christmas.

Because of the accident we did not make it to Wichita and the job evaporated. My uncle on my father's side came to get us, and we ended up staying with my paternal grandmother, the mean old blue and grey woman. My mother worked as a waitress until we could get back on our feet. Fortunately for Red and me, the old hag complained about too many mouths to feed and we ended up back at the Duffy Place, the safe place where my two heroes, Teddy and Billy  lived with hound dogs, fuzzy baby chickens, and pet raccoons.

# - 16-
## I NEVER DRINK SEVEN-UP

Nearing the bottom of the barrel with no job and no money, we moved into one of the low-priced cotton shacks. Normally used by migrant workers during the cotton harvest, these road-side shacks were nothing to brag about. In fact, they were clap-board wood frame houses positioned on either side of a central bathroom or bathhouse.

Red and I attended the first grade and kindergarten at a nearby Catholic orphanage that allowed children in the area to attend. As you might imagine, the teachers all wore habits. Having never seen a nun before, we were quite baffled by their attire. It certainly didn't take long to find out they had no patience for foolish children who expressed curiosity about their attire. More importantly, we were sternly admonished to sit quietly and only speak when spoken to.

Neither of us were good at sitting quietly, and it wasn't long before I got myself and the girl sitting next to me in trouble. Unfortunately, no infraction went unpunished. After they swatted the backs of our hands with the edge of a ruler, they tossed us into a dark and dusty book storage room. The girl's name was Dorothy; they called her Dot. She was a small frail girl and she began crying the minute the nun called her out. By the time we reached the book room she was sobbing convulsively, unable to catch her breath. Not realizing her punishment wasn't over, I didn't understand her all-consuming fear. I held her until she quit sobbing. It was then she shared with me the ugly truth; her punishment was not over.

She would not be allowed to eat the evening meal and would be required to kneel and pray for forgiveness until bedtime. Additionally, I was surprised to learn she did not have parents. Moreover, I didn't realize most of the kids in our class didn't have parents and lived at the school full-time. My first exposure to religion was not, by any stretch of the imagination, positive. Our uniformed classmates were not allowed to play creatively or develop their minds by interacting with educators. Instead they lived in fear, afraid to speak out or ask questions. Under the guise of education these children were warehoused until they aged out of the system, at which time they were not ready to become productive members of society. With almost no social skills and no technical skills, these functionally illiterate young adults were destined to end up wards of another state-run institution.

Finally, the long day at the children's prison ended, and we joined with a few local children. Much to the chagrin of the resident children, we were allowed to leave their hell hole. When we got home Dad had already eroded deeply into a bottle of whiskey and had no interest in knowing about our first day at the prison. Therefore, I didn't tell him or my mother about the incident in the book room or about my girlfriend Dot. In fact, we knew we were in for a long night and rushed outside to keep from being targeted as he nurtured his anger and insanity with strong drink.

Red and I were creative players and made a conscious effort to stay outside until Mother came home. Knowing we could look forward to a warm hug from our poor, bone-tired mother returning home to a prodigious alcoholic after working a twelve-hour shift. Unfortunately, she could look forward to the nightly rendition of recriminations and just plain cruelty from a chemically insane man.

While exploring the shower house Red realized we could plug the shower drain and six inches of water would accumulate on the cement floor. As the water accumulated around us, we pulled off our shoes and clothes, hung them on the hooks by the door, and began gliding around on the flooded floor. Red became the alligator. Roaring and propelling himself with his arms, he began chasing me around the room. I found safe haven on the toilet stool and sprinted around the room, teasing the gator and returning to the safety of the stool. On one such foray into the gator pond, giggling because of a close call, I leaped for the stool and missed the mark. My foot slipped off, and instead of rising up on the stool lid defiantly, I planted my face on the edge of the lid. Dazed from the blow, I rolled over to find Red's face crossed with fear. I could see the blood running down my chest, and he said he could see my teeth under my lip. He helped me dress, and we ran for the house, while blood soaked my favorite shirt.

Fortunately for us, not so much for her, my poor tired mother was returning home from work and we ran to the car. She took one look at me and pulled me into the car. Parting the wound she realized I was cut all the way through my bottom lip and we were off to the hospital. Unfortunately, my mother tended to panic when she saw her children battered and bleeding. With gravel flying and without looking she pulled out in front of a pickup truck. Reacting quickly, the driver took to the ditch to avoid a nasty wreck. My mother stopped at the filling station on the way to town to get directions to the hospital. The station attendant, whom she bought gas from in one to three-dollar increments, came bouncing out to the car to flirt with her as usual. Seeing a bleeding, sobbing child in her lap, he quickly directed her to a nearby regional clinic. We arrived, screeching to a halt in the middle of the parking lot. My mother and I, sobbing profusely, were directed to the emergency reception area. The doctor assured my mother it was not a serious injury and promised her my loose teeth would tighten up over time. The receptionist took her hand and led her to the reception area.

With the help of his pretty, young nurse, the doctor began deadening the margins of the gash below my lip. I remember the bright light and his conversation. "Will you remove the paint chips and irrigate while I prepare the sutures?"

"Yes, doctor."

"I will repair the mucosa first. Pull the lip up for me, that's it."

I drifted away as the mild sedative took effect. I felt a pulling sensation as the stitches were administered. Awakened by my mother's sweet voice, "The doctor is done, you're all stitched up. Just look." Gazing in a mirror, at my mother's urging, I thought the stitches were pretty cool.

The doctor came into the reception area and asked, "When was his last tetanus shot?" The answer of course was never. In 1955 tetanus vaccines contained the bloodserum of horses. The doctor explained that reactions to the vaccine were quite common and the procedure was to conduct a sensitivity test to check for a reaction. I went with the doctor, and within minutes he applied the few drops of the vaccine to a spot he scraped on my back. My tired and beleaguered mother got the news, "Well, he is reactive. We're in for a long night. He will be receiving a minute quantity of the vaccine every hour until he has received ten doses." Can you imagine a doctor who would spend ten hours diligently helping a small boy, knowing full well, his mother, still in her waitress uniform, would not be able to pay for his services?

While the doctor sutured my lip back together, my honest, forthright Mother quietly told the receptionist she would need to pay for the doctor's services over time, explaining to them, "I will get you paid. I pay my debts. I have a job." The receptionist responded, "Let's not worry about that right now honey, we will work with you. Let's worry about your son for now."

The doctor let my mother and I use the couch in his office where we restlessly slept in one hour increments for the next ten hours. My mother would wake me every hour, "Wake up, son, it's time."

I'd begin blubbering, "No, no, not again."

The doctor would administer the vaccination as gently as possible and say, "There you go. Now go back to sleep, we're almost done."

Finally, we were in the car on our way home. With the deadening long gone, my lip ached continuously with twinges of sharp pain which caused me to cry out. I didn't go to school that day and my mother didn't go to work either. My father had gone to apply for a job, and I got to spend a day with my mother who doted on me all day long. It was a great day.

My diligent and honest mother, true to her word, did exactly what she said she would do. Like clockwork, every other day she stopped by the clinic and shared the day's tips in an effort to defray her bill. In fact, spreading the day's tips out on the counter to count out half became so endearing, the receptionist who turned out to be the doctor's wife, tried to give Mother a discount. My mother vehemently refused, informing her, "I pay my bills. I'm not rich, but my word is good."

On the day of the final payment I was by her side to say 'thank you' and to show off my nicely healed lip. The doctor came out and got down on his knees to examine my lip one last time. "It has healed very nicely. You be more careful now, okay?"

I responded with a polite, "Yes, sir." The receptionist thanked my mother, gave her a final receipt and handed me a lollipop. Walking us to the door the nurse pulled my mother aside and said softly, "June, you can't coverup everything with makeup. I can find a shelter for you and your children." Mother declined with a smile, graciously accepted a hug, and we were out the door.

It was a good thing my mother was diligent about paying because we were going to need the doctor again. This time I really did it right. Playing in the warm spring rain, Red and I found a large puddle of water that had accumulated in a low spot by the back porch of the cotton shack and decided it would be great fun to make the four-foot jump from the porch into the pool. I rushed to be first—seldom did I get to be first at anything. I scooted under the pipe rail, looped my arms behind my back over the rail and paused to contemplate my landing.

With Red's urgings, "Go already," I made my leap and made a great two-point landing, not knowing there was a broken Seven-Up bottle sitting upright on its base lurking at the bottom of the inviting pool of water. I landed squarely on the bottle's jagged upright base and cried out in pain. Amazingly, the pain wasn't bad enough to keep me from clambering back up the steps for another turn. Red exclaimed, "You're bleeding." I looked down, and to my utter amazement my toes were turned the wrong way on the top of my foot. I knew I was in trouble. Red cried out, "Mother, help! Garry is bleeding!" Feeling weak in the knees, I sat down and stared at my backward toes. My mother scooped me up and bounded up the steps, grabbing a towel and the car keys. We were out the door and in the car before I knew it. Blood was spraying from the wound. My mother wrapped it tightly in a towel and admonished me to hold the towel tightly as we zoomed away.

Back at the clinic, the doctor unwrapped the towel carefully and exclaimed "Oh my God!"—the last thing you want to hear from your doctor. After bandaging it tightly with copious amounts of gauze until the bleeding stopped, he left the room quickly and returned a few minutes later. With a reassuring smile he told my mother, "I contacted a friend from medical school, a very skilled surgeon. This injury is too complicated for me to handle by myself. The foot is cut off at the ball, with tendon, vessel, and tissue damage that is beyond my skill to repair. My friend is on his way. Don't worry, we will take care of him." With that the nurse ushered my mother out of the exam room and gave me a mild sedative. Wrapped in a warm blanket, I fell asleep and awoke to find a shiny white cast on my foot and ankle. My mother wept softly as the surgeon explained, "I did my best tc reattach the tendons and vessels and reestablish the blood supply to his toes. With some luck, we won't lose any toes. However, due to extensive nerve damage the foot will be tender for mcnths, maybe years. Unfortunately, I don't expect him to regain full use of the foot. In fact, he will most likely have a lifelong limp."

Back at home we were greeted by my father, whom I was deathly afraid of and for good reason. Much to my surprise, he greeted me tenderly and without the strong smell of alcohol on his breath. He talked to my mother while I sat on his lap, afraid that any second his mood would change to abject anger as it frequently did. Instead, he assured me he would take care of me and that everything would be alright. For the next three days, he was a changed man. In fact, he carried me to the bathrocm and back without complaint, fixed peanut butter and jelly sandwiches for me, and even drew a cool airplane on my cast.

Ten days later, we returned to the clinic. The doctor sawed the cast off and smiled pleasantly at the healing that had taken place. He said, "Nice, very nice". He will need to remain in a cast for the next six weeks to be sure the tendons reattach. If there are no problems, I will see you in six weeks. Keep using the crutches and only touch the heel to the ground. Do not put any pressure on your toes."

Well, six weeks later, the cast came off and I stopped using the crutches. Determined not to limp, I fought through the pain. At the orphanage any display of weakness would get you abused by the older boys, and I wasn't about to limp in front of them. To this day I have a tender spot in the middle of the scar. However, I do not limp and have run marathons. No question, God put me in the way of a very skilled surgeon in 1955.

# THAT'S HOW HORSES LOOK

After only a few months attending the orphanage, we moved from the cotton shacks nearby to the town of Garland, Texas. Red and I were still in the first grade and kindergarten respectively. Without a doubt, we found a vastly different educational environment. The teacher actually seemed to like her job and the children in her classroom. The class was kindergarten through the third grade. We arrived as new students just two days before Saint Patrick's Day. My poor, hard-working mother was informed that Red and I would need tuxedoes and top hats to be leprechauns in the upcoming stage event. Having never seen a tuxedo up close, my mother, undaunted by the challenge, went to the local fabric store, where a pleasant surprise awaited her. Not only did the store's owner know what fabrics she would need, she had a pattern to follow. My mother set about cutting out the little jackets and stitching them together by hand, after which she made fine little felt top hats. Lo and behold, the next morning we were little tuxedo-clad leprechauns on our way to our first day at a new school. Of course Mother, who had worked through the night, was on her way to the café where she worked as a waitress.

When we arrived at our classroom, we were introduced to our classmates and promptly lined up with them to march to the auditorium for rehearsal. As the rehearsal unfolded we learned a song with the accompaniment of the mother of the prettiest girl in the class, Desdemona. Wow! Just her name made you look twice, and maybe she wasn't as pretty as her fabulous name. In any case, she wasn't hard to look at and the older boys wanted to call her 'girlfriend'. I was more interested in the monkey bars and kick ball.

Walking home from school we were suddenly attacked. A huge boy appeared out of nowhere growling and pawing at us with his huge hands. Suddenly I was on the ground and he was on top of me clawing at my body. His face was in mine, and despite the mask, I could smell his terrible breath. I began screaming and kicking as I tried to get away. Red jumped on him and began pummeling him with lefts and rights, causing him to roll off of me. I jumped to my feet and began banging him with my book bag while Red kicked him. To our amazement he flattened himself to the ground and began crying. We made a hasty retreat and ran all the way home. Upon regaling our story of the attack we received a skeptical gaze as neither of us were bruised, scratched, or injured in any way. My mother took time the next day to go to our school and report the incident. The principal smiled and said, "Your boys were in no danger; that boy is harmless. He is a retarded boy who lives just down the street. I will speak to his mother."

That evening just before supper, there was a knock at our door. When I opened it a thin unassuming woman with greasy blonde hair and a persistent downward gaze was standing on the porch holding hands with a giant boy, who hulked over her. Oddly, he was looking at the ground and never raised his head, even when his mother greeted us with, "He has come to apologize to you boys." He burst out a slurred and barely understandable, "I'm sully. I'm sully." I called for my mother, who appeared with spatula in hand. Seeing this odd pair she approached cautiously. "Can I help you with something?" The obviously embarrassed woman began to explain that her retarded boy was only playing and didn't intend to hurt us, and that he was sorry for scaring us. She bumped him with her elbow eliciting another round of "I'm sully. I'm sully." True to her nature, Mother said, "It's okay honey. My boys weren't hurt, but he really scared them." The hulking boy never looked up during the brief encounter on the porch. His mother assured us it wouldn't happen again. She smiled nervously, nodding as she turned to walk away. The hulking boy continued to look down as he lumbered next to his mother in an awkward shuffling gate. Having never encountered anyone who was retarded and fearing he would return, we quizzed Mother. She explained, "He isn't like you. His mind didn't develop properly, and though he has an adult body, in his mind, he is two years old."

Returning to school the next day, and after a successful dress rehearsal of the St Patrick's Day event, it was back to the classroom where we lined up to get name tags for our leprechaun attire to be hung neatly in the coat closet. Unfortunately, Red decided to antagonize me by telling me in front of everyone my name wasn't Garry; it was Garrett. I called him a liar and we went at it, cursing and pounding on each other. A credit to our hateful and angry father, by the time we were five we knew every curse word in the book and a good number of hateful and demeaning phrases. Much to the dismay of our teacher, we regurgitated every last one of them right there while rolling around on the floor, in front of God and everybody. All the while she stood over us saying, "Boys, boys! That's enough!" Consequently, on our second day at our new school we ended up in the principal's office where we got two licks each. Not exactly a glorious start by conventional standards, but we were unconventional boys and we found it laughable on the way back to class. That evening we walked back to school for the St. Patty's event. I was quite pleased to hold my mother's hand as we walked, in spite of being teased as a 'mama's baby'. The play went off without a hitch while we pretended to sing along, and my mother beamed with pride— certainly the prettiest woman in the crowd.

Upon returning home I began working on my homework. We were tasked with drawing our pet or an animal we liked. I chose the brown and white pinto horse in the small lot behind our house. To say I was observant with a keen eye for detail would be an understatement. In fact, I drew and colored this horse in finite detail, right down to the two-toned appendage hanging below his stomach. No question, the appendage overshadowed the entire drawing, and the blotch of tan in the middle of the white made it even more glaring. My mother must have choked back laughter as she admired my creation and patted me on the back. Proud as punch, I was off to school with my rendering of the pinto horse in hand. To my surprise, I was greeted with snickers when the other kids looked at my fine piece of art. When the sweet teacher pulled me aside to ask if I deliberately made a nasty picture, I had no idea what she was talking about. Fortunately, I think she believed me because I didn't get another trip to the principal's office. However, much to my dismay, my beautiful horse wasn't displayed on the blackboard with the other drawings. Instead, I was admonished to take it home, where my mother proudly displayed it on the refrigerator.

We had a huge black Labrador name Tubby. He lived in the house and was a wonderful playmate for two mischievous boys. We were warned about the protective and territorial nature of male dogs, and we were told to walk away from any confrontation between Tubby and other dogs in the neighborhood. Saying "Yes, we understand," we were off to play. Unfortunately, it didn't take long for one of the mean little bastards in the neighborhood to sic his dog on Tubby. The fight was on—our first dog fight was savage, bloody, and frightening. In a panic we ignored the instructions we were given, and we tried to break up the fight, which we found out later was tantamount to egging them on. Tubby finally prevailed. When we got back home with our poor dog, bloody and limping, we learned a lesson we would never forget. Our father took one look at the dog and said, "You didn't run away when the fight started did you?" When we answered that we tried to help him, he went into an uncontrollable rage.

Grabbing us by our arms, he began slamming us into one wall after another until we were barely conscious. Leaving us bruised and battered on the floor, he gathered up Tubby and headed to the nearby veterinary clinic. When he returned home, Tubby had several shaved spots on his body with white shiny stitches. We were ordered not to mention our punishment to our mother. He pulled us to his face by our collars, and glaring like a mad man, he demanded, "Do you understand me?" Oh yes, we understood quite well, as this was not our first beating. Later in the week, when the bruises appeared, we told our mother we were wrestling and rolled off the porch. We knew if we told the truth, their argument would escalate into a beating, and when he finished with our mother we would be next.

The sweet teacher made a practice of taking students home, in pairs, for dinner and an overnight stay. Everyone talked about what fun the sleepover was, especially in the company of their best friend. The teacher would fix a meal, read several chapters of the book of your choice from her library, and then it was off to bed after a warm shower. Red and I were a ready-made pair, and she invited us on a Tuesday night. We were so excited we could hardly contain ourselves during the school day. She had board games for us to play while she fixed the evening meal. And what a fabulous meal it was, fried chicken, macaroni and cheese, with peas and carrots. We ate with gusto and enjoyed every bite, except for the peas, but to be polite we choked them down and cleaned up our plates.

Showered and clean, we were ready for her to read a story as promised. Red picked a book, and she began to read. I don't recall the name of the book or remember anything about the story. However, I do remember how her expressive manner made the story come alive, and right then and there I fell in love with her.

When bedtime arrived, she escorted us to a room with two twin beds. Having never slept alone, I was quite excited. She told us to put on our pajamas and she'd come back and tuck us in. When we queried her about pajamas, she said, "Okay, just take off your clothes and hop in bed." Before she could leave the room, we stripped off our shirts and pants at which point, she exclaimed, "Where is your underwear?"

"Underwear? What's underwear?" we asked in unison. Without another word she whirled around and made a hasty retreat. Later that night I left my bed and crawled in with Red. Having your own bed wasn't all it was cracked up to be. In fact, it was cold and lonely.

## - 18 -
## THE FISH TRAP

My father had difficulty in social environments because of his PTSD, coupled with the fact that he was usually hungover, he had no patience for 'pin headed bastards' who wanted to know about his war experience. It was something he only talked about when he was sauced to the gills. He did not however have any problem in the woods or outdoors and was an accomplished hunter and fisherman.

Red and I watched from our shared bed as Mother rolled quietly down the driveway trying not to wake us. The restaurant where she worked attracted a good breakfast crowd, and the doors opened at 6:00 AM. In fact, she always said her best tips came from early risers. She was a petite woman and no doubt the prettiest waitress on staff, therefore her regular customers helped fill her tip jar. Certainly, with four hungry mouths to feed and a whiskey dependency to satisfy, she functioned as a pleasant and efficient waitress.

We rolled over and tried to sleep a little longer but the smell of coffee, oatmeal, and bacon waiting in the kitchen was more then we could resist. We stumbled to the kitchen, where Red reached up on his tiptoes to retrieve two bowls. I got spoons out of the drawer and brown sugar out of the cabinet, and we scooted together at the table. After applying copious amounts of sugar to make the oatmeal tolerable, we began eating and talking quietly about the day ahead.

We stopped talking and looked down when our father entered the room, scratching and groaning. We never knew what his mood would be like, especially in the morning. On this day he spoke to us kindly as he retrieved oatmeal and bacon from the stove. Though we loved bacon, we knew it was not for us and never touched a slice. He sat across from us as we ate in silence. Smiling, something that never seemed to quite fit his face, he said "Well boys we're going to build a fish trap today, hunt down a jackrabbit for bait, and put it in that big pond up north." We smiled and nodded cautiously, not knowing what might set him off. We learned not to respond unless he asked a direct question. He looked at us with a vexed expression and asked, "Well what do you think? Do you want to help?" He swizzled down his last bit of coffee, and we responded, "Yes, we will help."

We dressed for the cool weather and followed him to the shed. He pulled out a roll of chicken wire and a remnant of reenforcing wire and went about determining the circumference of the trap. He began scribbling on the door facing, mumbling, "pi R squared." And within a few seconds he said, "Seven and one-half feet." After cutting the reinforcing wire to length, he went about forming it into a circle by bending and wrapping the cut ends over the other edge. He pulled the wire together and secured it with several wraps, then continued the process at every four-inch juncture for the full length. Next, after scribbling on the door face again, he measured out two equal lengths of chicken wire and formed them into cones securing them at several junctures along their length with an odd-looking plier like device and circular pieces of metal he found in a small green and red cardboard box. He held up the device and asked if we knew what it was. Of course, we had no idea. He smiled and said, "It is a hog ringer." Pinching a metal ring between his fingers he said, "They clamp this into their noses to keep them from rooting under the fence." After securing the two cones onto each end of the wire cage with the small ends facing inward, he covered the trap with chicken wire. While cutting a trap door at the top with a copious number of hog rings placed around three sides to hold the wire together, he formed a hinge by not fully closing the rings on one side. He began explaining the functionality of the trap explaining, "They will enter the trap here and here. Once inside, they aren't smart enough to swim up and back through the narrow end of the cone." He went on, "My brother Gene showed me how to build this trap. He put his in the river, but it should work just as well in a pond."

With the trap setting ready, he secured his .22 automatic, and with the two of us in tow we were off to dispatch a jackrabbit for bait. After what seemed like several miles, he kicked up a rabbit. He fired in rapid succession at the fleeing critter, using the poofs of dust to adjust his aim. After eight or ten shots, adjusting forward with each shot, he finally rolled the fleeing rabbit with a lethal shot. He sent Red and I to secure the prize from the long grass where it laid, squirming in the final throes of death.

Walking back, Red and I shared custody of the jackrabbit. Unfortunately, our upbeat attitude began to wane as the conversation changed. Speaking to me, my father said, "You know you were named for my friend Garrett? The damned krauts got him," he sighed. "If I only had more ammo." We knew instantly the flashbacks were coming on and he would be self-medicating in no time. We disappeared as he began skinning the rabbit and we stayed out of sight the rest of the day. He was passed out when Mother got home and we were admonished to be quite as we ate supper and went to bed before he awoke.

Hearing the car crackle down the drive the next morning, we laid awake wondering what mood our father would be in. The day started out on an unpleasant note when he entered the kitchen growling, "Where is your mother?"

"She left for the café," we said in unison as he poured himself a cup of coffee.

He sat down across from us and glared, "What are you looking at?"

We answered, "Nothing," and made a quick exit.

We spent another day in hiding as he finished off a bottle of whisky. Fearing his wrath, lunch came and went, as it frequently did without a bite to eat. That evening was somewhat uneventful as my mother returned home with a fresh bottle. Pulling on it rapidly he passed out on the couch early and we went to bed without incident.

The next morning, he entered the kitchen in a pleasant mood. While eating his breakfast he said, "Well the jackrabbit should be ripe enough to attract fish. Will you boys help me put the trap in the pond?"

Smiling with anticipation we answered, "Yes, sir."

Pulling down the stinky, fly-blown rabbit, he laughed as we held our noses and backed away. Rifling through the reenforcing rod in the back of the shed, he found one the right size for the trap. He explained, "I need you boys to push this rod in through one of the cones. I will impale the rabbit and push the rod out the other end. One of you will need to hold it on that end." We did our part, gasping as the rod made an ugly grinding sound when he pushed it through the rabbit from back to front.

With the bait secured in the center of the trap, it was off to the pond. We walked along the shoreline until he found a suitable deep edge that the cattle were not using. With a length of reenforcing rod pushed into the soft wet ground, he waded out chest deep into the water and lowered the trap gently down. He tied a rope to the anchor and said, "We should have a trap full of fish by tomorrow morning."

The next day, brimming with anticipation, we were up early and got to spend some time with our mother while she fixed breakfast and dressed for work. To our amazement and utter relief our father awoke with a gleam in his eye. "This is catfish day boys. Are you ready?" We each carried a bucket as we marched along behind him, eager to see the results of his trapping efforts.

Standing by the stake as he hauled the trap to shore, we could see movement in the muddy water. And lo and behold, the trap was brimming full of wriggling catfish. Pulling the trap onto its side, he ordered us to bring the buckets. Laughing proudly, something we seldom heard, he began to fill our buckets with fish. He identified each one as he pulled them out. "This long-speckled fellow is a channel cat. They're fine eating. This green and yellow guy is a mud cat. They're not worth eating; throw this one back." When I reached for it, he admonished me to watch out for the fins on the sides and the one on its back. "Those fins are dangerous! Stick your thumb in his mouth, and don't get finned." With the trap emptied, we were on our way back home with not one, but two buckets full of speckled beauties. Red and I shared the load of one bucket with our hands joined together on the handle.

Back home with our bounty, we watched our father follow Mom's process for cleaning catfish—with one exception. After skinning, he fileted the meat off of the bone leaving a fine light pink strip of boneless meat. When Mother got home from work she was happy to find a bowl full of catfish filets resting in cool water in the refrigerator. She quickly changed clothes and began preparing a skillet of lard and the catfish for frying. I offered to help and began dredging the filets into flour until they were completely covered. Without a doubt, a skillet full of sizzling catfish elicits a smell finer than the sweetest of flowers.

We sat down to a table of fresh fried catfish, brown beans, and steaming baked corn bread. I always hurt after I ate. However, this time my overfilled stomach ached while I ate. No question, it was the most enjoyable meal I had ever eaten. My father came into the kitchen while we helped my mother with the dishes. He said, 'You know, that pond is full of clams. What say tomorrow we all go to the pond and boil clams over a wood fire?" My mother was agreeable and we were excited beyond belief. It seemed our life was changing as our father seemed to be recovering from his sadness concerning the war. My mother even said as she tucked us into bed "I think your father is getting over his regrets from the war." We didn't know what was happening but two good days in a row was a rarity, and it appeared we were about to have a third.

The next day we made our way to the pond as a family. A cool chill came over Red and I as we saw the neck of a whiskey bottle protruding from one of the grocery sacks. Clams in a pile, the water boiling, and the bottle cracked open, we knew what was coming. When the clams emerged from the boiling water, their shells were miraculously opened, revealing their pail white bodies. He scooped one up, poured out the milky liquid, shuffled it from one hand to another until it cooled, and tossed it into his mouth. "Mmm good" he said, "get one out for these boys."

Unfortunately, we found their shape and look disagreeable and were reluctant to eat them. He scolded us sternly and ordered us to try one. We knew that tone of voice, and staving off our desire to run away, we choked down the slimy half-cooked bivalves, one after another in an effort to keep him, now well-pickled, from boiling over.

He slapped my mother for saying they weren't done and we vaulted to our feet and made a hasty retreat to our hiding place in the barn. Unfortunately, the three-day streak of happiness ended with an explosion of anger and abuse. We heard our mother calling our names in the dark and we responded with a whispered, "We're over here." She hugged us and said it was safe to come in and go to bed. She had that copper stench about her, and we knew she had endured another beating. She must have been right about the clams because we all suffered from stomach cramps and diarrhea throughout the night and into the next day.

# 19

# THERE WERE RATS IN THAT HOUSE.

After several failed attempts to hold down a job, my father followed Coyote's lead and rented an old dilapidated farmhouse. The first night we were awakened by a thumping noise, which turned out to be rats bumping down the stairs. Our father said that based on their droppings they were big ones. Worse, the following night Red and I received nasty bites from the aggressive rodents.

My father decided he could build an electric trap to kill the giant critters and set about making a contraption. First, he built a square wooden frame and glued on screen wire that he salvaged from an old window screen in the barn. Next, he drilled and glued three-inch tall wooden pegs to the frame. Then, he reprovisioned thin copper wire from an old clock motor and attached it to the wood pegs. Finally, he cut the plug wire off the old clock, stripped the wires, and soldered the hot wire to the screen base and the neutral to the elevated wire. Plugging it into the wall, he tested the voltage with a meter. "Yup, 120. That should do the job." We were told how dangerous the trap was and admonished not to touch it.

That night, the trap baited with a dollop of peanut butter was placed on the kitchen floor, plugged in and ready for action. We couldn't wait for the results and fell into a restless sleep. Awakened by a painful bite, I cried out. Red and I launched out of bed to destroy the bruiser. Securing our wooden clubs which were leaning at the head of our mattress resting on the hardwood floor, I went for the light switch. *Click*. No light. With visions of rats all around us we made a hasty retreat to our shared bed where we banged our sticks on the floor until the scurrying noises subsided.

The next morning in the kitchen, sure enough there was a dead rat laying across the elevated wire of the trap. He was partially roasted and smelled to high heaven. Unfortunately, the electrocution had blown a fuse—meaning, for each rat caught a new fuse would be required. Realizing it would be cheaper to buy traditional wooden traps, my mother came home with three wooden spring-loaded rat traps.

The rats were giant, slick-tailed Norwegian rats, fast on their feet and strong. These were not scurry-away rats, but the kind that would jump at you and hiss when cornered. Unfortunately, the traps would neither kill them nor hold them for long. Therefore, Red and I, armed with elm sticks, were on rat duty. With such an important assignment we laid awake and listened for the snap of the trap and the squealing and scurrying noise the rats made as they tried to escape.

*Snap*! Another rat. We were up and bounding down the stairs to dispatch the ugly, struggling critter. Finding him under the table, we had to get down on our knees to whack him with our sticks. Of course, the commotion woke Mother who threw the rat, trap and all, out the back door and ordered us back to bed. We repeated the bludgeoning process night after night until ten or twelve rats had been successfully removed from the house. Finally, we were no longer awakened with nasty bites, and the stairs remained quiet.

A few weeks later we were both given bright, shiny BB guns. *Wow! If only we had rats to pursue.* We were given a lengthy session on gun safety and accurate shooting. Our father said "These are guns, not toys. They can kill small animals and cause serious injury to you boys. Never point them loaded, or unloaded, at anything you don't intend to shoot." We were also told not to shoot an animal we did not intend to eat. We shot bottles, cans, fence posts, and a square target that allowed us retrieve and reuse the BBs.

One day, seeing a barn swallow on the electric line some distance away, I couldn't resist the challenge. *Could I hit him that far away, or would he fly away unscathed?* I learned my shooting accuracy lessons well. Taking careful aim by bracing against the house and adjusting upward for the distance, I pulled the trigger. *Poof!* Feathers flew, and the beautiful black and orange bird fell to the ground. I was aghast at what I had done. I never expected to actually hit the mark.

Upon retrieving him I felt a plethora of emotions, pride for the successful shot, shame for having killed such a beautiful creature, but mostly fear of getting caught. I had committed the cardinal sin of killing a living creature I did not intend to eat. I ran behind the barn where with burgeoning shame for the dreadful act I buried him in a shallow grave. When I visited the grave the next day I was surprised to find it empty with feathers strewn about by some creature, that had eaten him, most likely a barn cat. I got away with the dastardly deed without punishment. However, the recrimination and guilt I felt was more than sufficient to deter me from ever doing that again.

# 20

# THE ESCAPE

Tubby, our black Labrador Retriever, quickly became our best friend. In fact, he became very protective of Red and me and would accompany us everywhere we went, even to our hiding place under the bed when nightly tirades began.

On a particularly bad night, Red and I finally got up enough nerve to go to our mother's rescue. I think we were six and seven. After finding out at school that not all fathers beat their wives and children, we realized that we should try to help our mother. That night, the beating started because the rent was past due, and the owner came to attempt to collect it. My mother made the mistake of mentioning that there was a job opening at the filling station. He flew into a rage at the demeaning nature of the job and accused her of trying to humiliate him. When he started hitting her we panicked and ran to our hiding place under the bed. Red began saying that we should help her and that hiding was wrong. Finally, although we were about to pee our pants, we went into the living room to try to intervene. He had his back to us. We each picked up one of our toys. We yelled, "Stop hurting her!" And we struck out. I hit him with my fire truck and Red did the same with a yellow dump truck.

What a mistake. He turned and grabbed us by our arms and began to slam our skinny little bodies together and continued until my mother jumped on him from behind and bit his ear. He dropped us to the floor, barely conscious, and began to beat our mother with renewed fervor. She screamed at us to hide and we flew from the room, bleeding and crying. Tubby joined us with reassuring licks and warm affection and we piled up on him and listened in tears as our mother took the brunt of his anger for jumping on his back to allow us to escape. The fighting sounds of anger and abuse subsided and suddenly the door opened with a bang. "Where are you little bastards? I wasn't through with you." In the darkness he reached aimlessly under the bed and grabbed Red by the leg. When Red cried out Tubby reacted with a guttural growl, which prompted a response of "God damned dog!" Then our father quickly released Red and left the room. We were so proud of Tubby. Finally, we had a protector.

Unfortunately, because of us, Mother received one of the worst beatings of her life, and we knew we were the cause. That night she did not come in to let us know she was okay and to tuck us into bed. In fact, we finally fell asleep under the bed with Tubby between us. We awoke with the earnest fear that our mother was dead—the worst feeling I have ever experienced.

We found her, too badly beaten to stand, and did our best to help her. Finally, she was able to stand and move about with our help. When we told her about Tubby's protective behavior she responded, "That's not good." We puzzled as to why that could possibly be bad but we never asked.

The next day, hung over and angry, our father informed us that he needed to tie the dog up because he had become dangerous. Lashed to a post outside we were admonished to stay away from him. Midday, to our amazement he took Tubby some fresh raw hamburger which our good boy promptly ate with gusto. Tubby remained outside when Red and I went to bed. The next morning, he was gone.

We were told he had escaped in the night and run off. We walked in the woods all day long and called him… to no avail. The next morning our father informed us that he had found him and led us to the place where he laid in a hollow log, informing us that the farmer had likely poisoned him for chasing cattle. We cried ourselves to sleep that night. We knew Tubby didn't chase cattle. Red hugged me and said, "Don't say anything, but I'm sure he killed him because he was afraid of him." At that point my fear of our father turned into abject hatred and I vowed to get even. In fact, we talked about ways to kill him. No question, when you are subjected to anger and violence you begin to internalize them as a solution to your problems and it begins early.

We lived in the middle of nowhere so there was no help available for our family. The beating had taken place on a Saturday; therefore, by Monday Mother was able to get around well enough to leave for work. When we arrived to the Duffy Place, where she planned to leave us for the day, her brother Billy took one look at the three of us and argued with renewed insistence—finally convincing her that she had to get out before he killed one of us.

When the time came Billy arrived to help us escape, sometime around midnight. We didn't have a phone so he parked down the road and snuck up and watched the house. When he was sure the raging was over he pecked quietly on the window. My mother coaxed us out from under the bed and admonished us to be quiet. She told us we were leaving with Billy and we wouldn't be coming back. She had packed bags and hid them under her bed. With our few possessions in hand, we were afraid to even breathe as we made our way out of the dark house and down the road where Billy had parked.

Billy had two sacks of groceries and twenty dollars to help us get started. We drove in the night for hours to a strange white two-story apartment. Billy had taken a day off work to locate it and to pay the first month's rent. The apartment had two beds. However, we all slept in one bed that first night and were happy to be there.

My mother, the bravest person I have ever known, escaped in the night with three kids, one in diapers, with twenty dollars in her pocket and two sacks of groceries. She had one month to find a job or be evicted.

That morning she went outside to look around and there it was, the More Burger, on the highway not two blocks away. Determined to find work, she crossed Stillwater Creek on a twelve-inch sewer pipe. Still bruised from the last beating she pleaded for work. Fortunately, God put her in the way of a good and kind man who not only gave her a job on the spot, but gave her an advance on her pay, a sack of hamburgers for two little turd-hammers, and a reassuring hug.

The guilt for causing her to receive one of the worst beatings of her life subsided. For me, it was later in life when I realized our feeble but brave attempt to rescue her served to escalate matters to the point she came to the realization that she had to save her children. God blessed my 5' 2" mother with uncommon bravery and an exceedingly strong will to survive. And survive we did.

Red and I had to take care of our baby sister so Mother could work. Fortunately, during slow periods at the More Burger my mother would cross the creek on the sewer pipe and check on us. Those were good days. My stomach quit hurting except when I ate because I always overate when we were fed. And we were able to fall asleep in our shared bed instead of under it. Mother was happy too, and we bathed in the sound of her sweet voice as she rocked and sang our baby sister to sleep.

## - 21 -
## THE MAGIC CAT

Living in the shadow of the More Burger gave my mother peace of mind for the first time in almost a decade. As for Red and me, we began to explore and become acquainted with our new surroundings when we weren't caring for our baby sister while Mother worked as a carhop. With a running creek a few yards away we were in little-boy heaven—until the resident bully paid us a visit. Boy was he in for a surprise! Hardened by the violent years, we dispatched him quickly.

The day before he showed up, we found a stray black kitten. We fed him all the cornflakes and milk he could eat which promptly gave him terrible diarrhea. The poor cat had the runs so bad he squirted when you squeezed him. That same afternoon the bully returned with his older brother. Now this boy was a big, ugly bruiser with a speech impediment that made him humorous even when he was threatening to pull your head off. We evaded his first awkward run at us and bolted upstairs and into the apartment. We weren't satisfied just to have outwitted him, so we opened the window and began taunting the two of them. With our coaxing, they were finally in just the right place directly under the window. We stuck the cat out and gave him a squeeze. Before they realized what was happening, a sheet of nasty cat poop shot across their faces and shoulders. The older one stepped back, and with eyes bulging, he looked like he was going to explode. And boy did he explode—with a blast of vomit that hit his brother squarely on the back of his neck prompting him to follow suit. We laughed until we cried watching them on the ground heaving up their breakfasts. Without another word they ran home. Of course, we knew they'd be back.

Unfortunately, we didn't live on Stillwater Creek for long. The monster we knew as our father found us and we had to escape to another home. My mother lost her job. More than likely she quit because she didn't want to further endanger anyone at the More Burger. I guess he made an ugly scene when he bloodied my mother's nose and got his crazy, drunken ass arrested. Consequently, we had time to escape to a rotten old duplex where she encountered a new friend, Ruby who became our babysitter. Appropriately named for a gem, she was a drop-dead gorgeous half-Cherokee woman with beautiful tan skin, high cheek bones, full lips, long flowing jet-black hair, and piercing water-blue eyes. Too young to appreciate her form I watched men, even those in the company of their wives, turn for a second look as the gem passed by. She was truly a sight to behold. She was married to a brilliant, diligent man, who while working on his engineering degree, labored nights to support her and their two girls. As one might expect, she also had a boyfriend who would spend days in her apartment swapping gum and grubbing right in front of us.

Certainly, we got an unwarranted look at illicit sex, which we found very confusing and intriguing.

The boyfriend took it upon himself to teach me a lesson for being disobedient. Pulling off his belt, he came for me. I went quickly out the door, down the stairs, and around to the garage below, which contained piles of gunnysacks full of pinecones. He pursued me with great anger and prodigious cursing. I evaded him with ease. In fact, it became a game, as I cursed back and laughed at him. Sweaty and frustrated, he finally gave up and went back to the gem in the apartment next door. After we gave my mother an account of the day's events, loaded for bear, she made it abundantly clear that he was to stay away from her children and there would be no more gum swapping in front of us.

With the gem and her boyfriend busy, we had time to explore the neighborhood and get acquainted with the neighbor kids. There was a laundry not two blocks away, where an extended family lived. There was a grandma, a feisty, old alley cat of a woman, who drove us away with "You kids get the hell out of here! We're trying to run a business!" Her grandchildren flew out the side door and began to threaten us with a beating. Without further ado, the fight was on. Though we were smaller, we quickly sent them back through the side door crying. Two days later here they came with the neighborhood bully, three years older and two heads taller. He held us down while the laundry mat boys pummeled us. A lesson learned, never stand up to older, bigger, stronger boys or the little bastards who pay them as mercenaries.

After a long, stormy night which elicited three to four inches of rain, Red and I found the six-foot ditch across from the apartment brimming full of fast-flowing water. Always ready for another adventure, we stripped down to our tighty-whities and jumped into the fast-flowing water. *Wow!* It was great fun. We ducked under the plank bridges across the ditch and popped up on the other side. One trip down the half-mile run wasn't enough. We ran back and started our second run, laughing and giggling the whole way. Rocketing down the ditch for a second time, we realized a police car was driving next to us. We weren't doing anything wrong. What did they want.

When we reached the area where the ditch flattened out, we pulled ourselves out and walked up to the car. The biggest, scariest policeman said, "What are you boys doing? You could become tangled under one of those bridges and drown. Where do you live?" We pointed to the two-story sand rock apartment building. Ordering us into the car, we were driven back and admonished to put our clothes back on. Ruby was summoned to the door with the loud knocking of a night stick on the door frame. The jewel appeared with, "Good morning, officers. Are these boys in trouble?" She leaned down to pat me on the head as her well-formed breasts, unencumbered by foundation, pushed forward and filled the V of her V-neck shirt. Instantly the demeanor of the policemen changed.

All smiles, they replied, "No ma'am, they're not in trouble. When we saw them swimming in that fast-flowing ditch, we were worried for their safety."

Ruby responded, "Oh my, they were in that ditch across the street?"

"You need to watch these boys more closely. They could have drowned if we hadn't stopped them."

Ruby offered, "Thank you officers for saving my boys."

Smiling ear to ear the two officers responded, "You're welcome. You have a good day now." We gained a new respect for Ruby when she looked over her shoulder as she bounded up the stairs and said, "I won't tell if you won't."

# - 22 -
## CONCLUSION

Life, in more cases than not, is unfair and unpredictable. My mother broke the cycle of abuse in time for Red and me not to end up as abusive husbands ourselves. We were however left with PTSD from the violent years. Neither of us are socially adept, and we both have problems with authority. No question, Red saw more abuse and was impacted by it 18 months longer than I was. Therefore, his PTSD is somewhat more severe. He was never able to put it in a place that allowed him to become a fully functional member of society. He went from one job to another with little success, until he found a job as a bounty hunter. The job was all-consuming, and coupled with the element of danger, it kept his mind busy and moderated his PTSD. Also, it allowed him to feed his need to rescue women and children who were being abused.

I had many jobs before I found computer science and became a software engineer. I found my attention to detail and my love of solving puzzles made me a perfect candidate for the software world. And I loved every minute of my career at one of the big five oil companies. In fact, I was successful beyond my wildest dreams. I was fortunate enough to marry a kind and tolerant woman who put up with me for 47 years. Unfortunately, it took me 20 years to trust her with the story of my early childhood years.

I have painfully little wisdom to impart based on my dubious upbringing and my struggles to find my way in life. I do know, without question, nothing is more important than to love and be loved. Everything else is ephemeral. Certainly, no greater love exists than love born of sacrifice. It was through the self-sacrifice and strength of my mother's love that I survived the first six years of my life. I will never forget the relief I felt holding her hand as we escaped in the night. Later in life, I realized the gravity of her bravery as she marched into total uncertainty with a single goal in mind, to save her children.

# DEDICATION

*This book is dedicated to the memory of my sweet mother who found the bravery to rescue me from an impossible situation.*

www.ingramcontent.com/pod-product-compliance
Lightning Source LLC
Chambersburg PA
CBHW031307060726
47590CB00003B/1100